FROM WEST LANCASHIRE

Edited by Lynsey Hawkins

First published in Great Britain in 2000 by
YOUNG WRITERS
Remus House,
Coltsfoot Drive,
Woodston,
Peterborough, PE2 9JX
Telephone (01733) 890066

HB ISBN 0 75431 852 4
SB ISBN 0 75431 853 2

FOREWORD

This year, the Young Writers' Future Voices competition proudly presents a showcase of the best poetic talent from over 42,000 up-and-coming writers nationwide.

Successful in continuing our aim of promoting writing and creativity in children, our regional anthologies give a vivid insight into the thoughts, emotions and experiences of today's younger generation, displaying their inventive writing in its originality.

The thought, effort, imagination and hard work put into each poem impressed us all and again the task of editing proved challenging due to the quality of entries received, but was nevertheless enjoyable. We hope you are as pleased as we are with the final selection and that you continue to enjoy *Future Voices From West Lancashire* for many years to come.

CONTENTS

Kimberley Wright	68
Natalie Buschini	69
Laura Chadwick	70
Michelle Armstrong	70
Richard Turek	71
Natalie Gornall	72
Laura Cullen	73
Sarah Sumner	74
Liam Kilgallon	75
Natina Cookson	76
Michelle Fulton	77
Jade Wood	78
Madeline Reed	79
Michael Wright	80

Fleetwood High School

Caroline Reid	81

Glenburn High School

Leah Rendall	82
Claire Dreha	82
Anita Clegg & Anita Buckley	83
Samantha Williamson	84
Natasha Crangle	84
Krista Morgan & Tanya Curran	85
Laura Elms	86
Mark Newby	87
Stephen Bristow	88
Stephanie Dreha	88
Philip Finegan	89
Ian Smith	90
Toni Bell	90
Colin Malone	91
Hollie Gelhardt	92
Michelle Wearing	92
Kimberly Rowlands	93
Helen Dumkow	93
Ian Rendall	94

Victoria Miller	94
Natalie Duggan	95
Shaun Neve	95
Helen Pulford	96
Adam Waite	96
Anthony Hoy	97
Stephen Borrows	97
Jenny Hays & Gemma Harrison	98
Nikki Shaw	98
Vincent Bennett	99
Samantha Baxter	100
Amy Hedges	100
Rebecca Harrison	101
Kev Dean	101
Lisa Stacey	102
Sarah Nixon	102
Samantha Kelly	102

Morecambe High School

Daniel Anderton	103
Pamela Slack	104
Kathryn Glover	105
Claire Flower	106
Katy Henderson	106
Jessica Uphill	107
Kylie Chapman	108
Laura Hodgson	108
Laura Devey	109
Ben Hill	110
Amanda Howard	110
Peter Donald	111
Rebecca Owen	112
Ben Henderson	112
William Gordon Mackenzie	113
Adam Ball	114
Rachael Stansfield	114
Amy Quesne	115
Helen Snape	116

The Poems

ONE OF THE BOYS

Look at the boys, I think they are funny
Some are fat and some are skinny,
I think they are fun to have around
But Mum keeps telling me they're out of bounds.

They laugh and joke and call me names
And sometimes they can be real pains,
They dress themselves up in designer gear
And think they are big drinking cans of beer.

They tease us girls about our clothes,
But we don't care, that's the way it goes,
They mess with their bikes and get dirty
With oil and sometimes they make my temper boil.

But they give motorbike backies just for a lark and
Whizz me around the deserted park,
Boys are much more fun, than silly toys
Yes! I'd like to be one of the boys.

Kristel Woodrow (12)

NIGHT SKY

Behind the mountains and down the cliff,
The sun sets sparkling in the mist.
After it's gone down something arrives,
A big silver ball in the sky.
What is this high and mighty thing?
It shines like a crown of a mysterious king.
Starting to climb towards the velvet black sky
Where little specks sparkle and twinkle in my eye.

Ashley Michelle Jones (12)
Burscough Priory High School

EVERTON FC

E ager to play they run out onto the pitch,
V arious players do their warm-ups,
E veryone cheers when the whistle is blown,
R unning with the ball the supporters all cheering,
T wisting and turning around all the defenders,
O n the ninth minute of play they shoot and miss,
'N ever going to score,' they all say.

F inally comes the end of the first half,
O ver half-time they have a team talk,
'O h dear,' the manager said, 'You're as clumsy as clowns.'
T hey all run out onto the pitch and then the whistle blows and
B efore you could say 'Everton FC'
A ll they did was score and score and score,
L eft and right,
L eft and right.

C ampbell kicked the ball and scored another goal,
L eft and right, left and right,
U nsworth kicked the ball and shot and scored,
B ut the whistle went just before it went in the net, oh well
  they won anyway.

Leslie Williams (12)
Burscough Priory High School

I AM FEELING BLUE

I am feeling blue and there's nothing to do,
Lying in bed scratching my head.
I am feeling blue and there's nothing to do.

I am feeling blue and there's nothing to do.
My mates are out running about.
I am feeling blue and there's nothing to do.

I am feeling blue and there's nothing to do.
My leg's in plaster, not another disaster.
I am feeling blue and there's nothing to do.

I am feeling red I am fine in my head.
I can't wait to get out and shout about.
I am feeling red I am fine in my head.

Jonathan Smart (12)
Burscough Priory High School

NIGHTCLUBBING

Hesitating at the door,
Too young, too young,
Heart overrules head.
In you go.
Don't think.

Inside, like a flood of unfamiliar faces,
They wait expectantly, oh, when will it start?
When it does, no one is prepared
For the throbbing, pounding, banging noise
That shatters windows and numbs brains.

Then like a rabble of music-starved youths,
They jump and wave and *move!*
Each absorbed in the pulsating beat.
Till it's past midnight, Mum's going to kill me!
But some go on dancing into the night.

Christine Felton (12)
Burscough Priory High School

SNOW

Cold, crisp and crunchy,
Snow is very cold,
If you go outside in winter,
You might have found it's snowed.

I like the look of cobwebs,
In the morning sun,
They're wrapped in their snow case,
Like a fresh iced bun.

When you fall over it isn't very nice,
But what you've probably slipped on,
Is a big hard patch of ice.

We build lots of snowmen,
We make them really big,
With a carrot for a nose and coal for eyes,
With arms made from twigs.

When it's all melted,
All the fun has gone,
We'll have to wait until next year,
There's always another one.

Adam Walsh (13)
Burscough Priory High School

MY GIRLFRIEND

My girlfriend,
is kind and courageous,
She is elegant and stylish.
And she would never tell a lie.

My girlfriend,
is great and graceful,
She is smart and sensible,
And she would never tell a lie.

My girlfriend,
is cute and cuddly,
And would never tell a lie.

My girlfriend,
is fun and frivolity
And she has told a lie!

Ross Tilley (12)
Burscough Priory High School

CATS

Cats are quiet
They come wild or tame
They are good for passing the blame.

Cats are good companions
They are always happy to see you
They're even your friends when you've got the flu.

Cats are very bright
They chase anything that wiggles
It always gives me the giggles.

Cats like to sleep a lot
They sleep in the funniest places
On the TV's one of the funniest cases.

Cats are friendly
They purr after a few strokes and pats
They sit on the comfy rug ready for you to come
And sit next to the brilliant cat.

John Eddison (13)
Burscough Priory High School

LIGHT, NO SIGHT

No sight,
Just light,
I am blind I cannot see,
I read with my fingers,
That's just for me,
No sight but light.

No sight,
Just light,
I have no colour,
Just many textures,
To adore,
No sight, but light.

No sight,
Just light,
I have no green,
I have no pictures,
To be seen,
No sight, but light.

No sight,
Just light,
It is as colourless as the air,
I'm a blind child,
This is quite rare,
No sight, but light.

No sight,
Just light,
It's special for me,
Because that's the way I am,
I only can't see.

It's *only* no sight, but there is light.

Lara Green (12)
Burscough Priory High School

WHO WANTS TO BE A MILLIONAIRE?

'Who wants to be a millionaire?'
I ask myself as I brush my hair.
I saw a programme on TV,
That gave a million away for free!
When I'm older
'bout 25
I plan to get a car and drive
Not a cheap one I must say
But from a wealthy man - who'll pay!
A millionaire, no, that's not right
A billionaire, that's got some bite
One who only thinks of me
Especially when having tea.
I asked a poor person in the street
If they would like to clean their feet
And become a millionaire
(something which indeed is rare)
Of course they did indeed say yes
They said they would like to become
someone who was not a bum
Anyway enough of that
Would you like to have a cat?
No, that's not right, listen to me
What would you like to be?
A millionaire?
A billionaire?
A willion-fillion-smillionaire?
I know what I want straight and clear
I want to keep some wild deer!

Lousie Elizabeth Heywood (12)
Burscough Priory High School

Trust Me I'm A Genius!

The square of the hypotenuse is equal to the sum of squares of the
other two sides.
Trust me I'm a genius!

The age of the Earth is approximately 2 billion years.
Trust me I'm a genius!

The quechua-languages play 'Ollantay' of the Inca of Peruis is
exclusively oral.
Trust me I'm a genius!

Quantum mechanics deals with statistical inferences relating to large
numbers and individual events.
Trust me I'm a genius!

The most important factors necessary to lower population growth rates
in the developing world are democracy and social justice.
Trust me I'm a genius!

In Athens in the fourth century BC, Ionian natural philosophies and
pythagorean mathematical, science combined to produce the syntheses
of the philosophies of Plato and Aristotle.
Trust me I'm a genius!

The writer of this poem is that *genuis* (oops!)

Lucy-Ann Duff (13)
Burscough Priory High School

At The Beach

The sun was floating in the sky,
Like a beautiful butterfly.
The sea was crystal clear,
While the fishermen were fishing on the pier.
The dolphins were dancing in the caves,
Like a bobbing boat on the waves.

The children were making sandcastles,
While the parents weren't getting any hassles.
I was swimming in the sea,
When a fish swam next to me.
A beautiful summer's day,
It's a pity it can't stay that way.

Melissa Elliott (12)
Burscough Priory High School

WINTER

Snow as thick as ice
And so cold falling on a garden
As white as rice
Snow floating down so soft and cold,
Falling on the grass covered in snow,
The sky so grey and bleary.
No rain or cloud,
Just snow and mist,
Snow falling on a garden
Floating down towards the fire,
Down, down and down it goes,
The snow starts melting
As it's coming down, down and down,
The grass, white, covered with snow,
Snow coming down, down, down,
Melting, melting and melting
And soon the fire goes out, out and out.

Amanda Joanne Gore (12)
Burscough Priory High School

BEAUTY

I wish I was upon a star,
A star high above the clouds floating,
In the heavens,
Like a swan on a flowing river,
The magic would make my eyes get bigger and bigger.
I know what I would like to do
That is to dance around the heavens
And sing like an angel
The fluffy white clouds would carry me far and beyond
As if I was riding a great white horse
Yes, that's what I'd like to do
When I eventually come down to Earth
I will be a peacock with its feathers
Spread out like a rainbow on a sunny day
I shall sing like a nightingale high in a tree for all to hear
I will pick a sweet-smelling rose from the garden of life
Yes, that is what I'd like to do

Anna Maria Panteli (12)
Burscough Priory High School

LIKE A STATUE

The lonely cat just sits there like a statue
Watching and waiting and hoping,
That someone will pick him,
Choose him.
Then a shadow falls over the cage,
Two people stop by the cage,
But they soon go to another cage.
The lonely cat just sits there like a statue.

The lonely cat just sits there like a statue
Still watching and waiting and hoping,
That someone will choose him.
Then two people stop by the cage,
His watching and waiting is now over,
The no longer lonely cat no longer sits there
Like a statue.

Rebecca Ward (12)
Burscough Priory High School

THE WRITER OF THIS POEM

The writer of this poem
Is taller than a giraffe
As timid as a mouse
As beautiful as can be.

Has red hair like a strawberry
She's as intelligent as a rocket scientist
Has blue eyes like the Pacific Ocean
Confident that day will turn to night.

As caring as a mother hen
As daring as a devil
As perfect as a peach
As cuddly as a teddy bear.

The writer of this poem
Never ceases to amaze
As one in a million billion
(or so the poem says.)

Rachael Louise Smith (13)
Burscough Priory High School

MY FUTURE

One day I hope that I will become a pop star.
I will play my own music in my new bright pink car,
I will perform in the stadium at Wembley,
And not in my school assembly.
Everybody will be telling me I'm really good,
And buying me a yummy chocolate pud.
I'll be on stage performing in front of all my fans
And after it's all over all I will see
Is thousands of hands.
They will be waving and screaming
Telling me they've enjoyed my show
Now I have to tell them it's time to go.

Abaigeal Wallace (12)
Burscough Priory High School

IN THE COUNTRYSIDE

The outsides are cold,
The wind never holds.

The trees line the sky,
As the birds go by.

The grass is green,
And is always seen.

The clouds are white,
And the stars shine at night.

The sun is yellow,
As the birds bellow.

Laura Ann Swift (12)
Burscough Priory High School

THE GHOST

Looking into the darkness
I saw a beautiful shining light
It totally overtook me
Because of its beautiful sight.

Then I saw this image
Walking towards my bed
It had a face like gold
And its clothes were silver-red.

I looked up and smiled
And it smiled back
And then I saw nothing
Because everything went black.

The next morning
Got out of bed to get the mail
But before I got downstairs
On the table was a lovely silver veil.

Claire Phillips (12)
Burscough Priory High School

SNOW

Snow is crunchy,
And very cold.
It melts into water,
And is too cold to hold.

Snow is white,
And also quite bright.
You'd better watch out,
It may give you frostbite.

Linzi Heaton (12)
Burscough Priory High School

THE MONSTER

A grey lifeless object
With a black patch on its head
It stood on an ocean of wood
Like a ship on a calm sea
A monster which conquered humanity
Suddenly the black patch came to life
A whirring clicking followed
A mouse scuttled across the wood
To a board covered in bumps
Then a flying saucer came
And flew into the monster's belly
The patch burst into multicoloured light
The patch as bright as the sun
The computer had come to life.

Peter Lewis (12)
Burscough Priory High School

UNDER THE SEA

Under the sea
Fishes live
Sharks hunt
Tiny fish hide inside shells
Oysters open and close
Dolphins jump out the sea
Sharks swim around for food
Eels hide inside shipwrecks
Fish coloured like the rainbow
Dodge around the seabed.

Rebecca Rowntree (12)
Burscough Priory High School

MY BRIGHT SILVER FRIEND

I had a good time yesterday,
Me and my silver friend
Went away.
We went up a hill
Right to the top,
And not once did we stop.
We saw a bright star,
Way up afar,
Gleaming like new,
Just like my silver friend . . . you.
My silver friend is?
I don't think you'll guess.
He is my brand new BMX.

James Evans (12)
Burscough Priory High School

LAZING ON HOLIDAY

Lazing on the water
looking up into the sky.
Listening to the waves splash
as the seagulls fly and swoop by.

As the sun is shining
looking onto the beach
I see lots of people having fun.

The sea is full of people swimming,
You can see lots of fish and coral.
It is an awesome sight.
This is my favourite place
Which gives me a lot of delight.

Matthew Blessington (13)
Burscough Priory High School

MY DOG TOBY

My dog Toby
has spots upon his back
he likes to chase the pussy cats
and then they chase him back.

My dog Toby
is only just a titch
he only has got little legs
but he can jump a ditch.

My dog Toby
sleeps upon the chair
he's very fond of chocolate
and is partial to a pear.

My dog Toby
is a little fat
but he can run rather fast
and even catch a rat.

My dog Toby
drives me round the bend
but my dog Toby
is my best friend.

Kevin Riley (12)
Burscough Priory High School

MY DAD

My dad is a very nice
man and is kind and
thoughtful to me.

He is as hard as a rock
and as cool as ice,
trustworthy he will always be.

He works as hard as a
dog, then sleeps like a log.
He likes a few beers
to drink with his peers.

My dad is a very nice man,
he is very special and
means a lot to me.

Anna Cain (13)
Burscough Priory High School

THE CLOCK MAZE

The clock hand ticks beside me,
I watch as it makes its way
Round and round,
Like it's lost in a never-ending maze,
Keeps following itself,
Though certain where it's going.

The alarm clock sounds,
Quiet but loud when it's quiet,
I rush my arm at it,
But knock it over,
I leap at it,
And the sound ends.

The clock is fully awake,
The clock never sleeps,
But over the years it sleeps
And everything stops.

Duncan McFarlane (12)
Burscough Priory High School

DERWENT WATER DREAM

The lake was a mirror reflecting the hills,
Boats merrily bobbing up and down,
While anchored in little peaceful bays,
Canoes hitting the waves from the ferries,
Boats go bounce, bounce, bounce.
Splash, splash, splash!
Some people swimming,
Some people canoeing,
Some people sailing,
The lake was a mirror reflecting the hills.

Christian Stott (12)
Burscough Priory High School

MY BEST FRIEND

My friend is as tall as a tree,
She has golden hair like the sun.

She runs as fast as the wind,
And she's as quiet as a mouse.

She's as skinny as a twig,
But she eats like a pig.

She's my best friend,
And I hope I am hers.

Sarah McNeill (12)
Burscough Priory High School

PHEOBE

I love Pheobe,
Pheobe is my dog
I'd be just as happy,
If Pheobe was a frog.
She runs around the garden,
Being really mad,
When I'm at school I miss her,
It makes me really sad.
Pheobe has a brother,
They're really like each other.
When I say 'You're a good girl,'
She gives me a twirl.
When I take her for a walk,
She likes to talk to other dogs.
     Woof!
       Woof!

Carla Keating (12)
Burscough Priory High School

MY BROTHER THE VAMPIRE

My brother is a vampire as ugly as a flea,
every time he bites you it feels like a bee,
you wouldn't really know this because you wouldn't see,
I think he's ruled by death
he smells like rotting corpses,
every time my mum said 'Bath' he would bite a leg,
I think it's really mean
he bit my dog last night, my mum says 'No pets now.'

Stuart Heron (12)
Burscough Priory High School

WINNING

Michael Owen, Andy Cole,
Never fail to score a goal,
Corners, free kicks, penalties,
Bring the fans down to their knees,
The kick of the boot,
The roar of the crowd,
But was it offside?
Was it allowed?
If you can't win the league,
And you've given up,
You can always win the
FA Cup!

Robert Jackson (12)
Burscough Priory High School

A BRAND NEW DAY

The sun is a shiny, golden ball,
Hanging in the sky.
The moon is a giant reflecting globe,
As it passes the sun by.
There is an instant darkness,
The sky is full of stars,
Which are like diamonds,
Glittering brightly from afar.
When the sun rises,
All the stars disappear,
It's a brand new day,
The morning is here!

Calum Kirby (12)
Burscough Priory High School

A HORSE OF THE NIGHT

This horse is like a wild, gentle bull.
He moves gracefully like a ballet dancer.
His black, shiny coat passes you like the night
His tail so soft, like velvet.

His eyes gleam as if he is in a photo,
His breathing makes a hot mist,
His hooves clang lightly on the road,
He gallops free like a breeze.

One minute past one and he has not yet gone,
He flies through the village every night.
He's not yet gone . .
Forty one minutes past one and he has finally gone.

He's back again in the midnight mist,
He runs down the country lanes,
Swift like an arrow reaching a target,
Peace at last, he has finally gone forever.

Nicola Bampton (13)
Burscough Priory High School

SNAKES

Snakes move with pride
Looking from side to side.
The scaly snake slithers
And slides, through the grass it glides,
Hunting for its prey
Make sure to stay out of the way.

Richard Taylor (12)
Burscough Priory High School

MY UNCLE DAVID'S CATS

My Uncle David and his cats have come to stay,
Our cat is thinking of running away,
They are big she is small,
Now she will only come when we call.

One is a tom and one is black,
Lucy thinks they might attack,
She eats their food when they're away,
Then she sleeps for the rest of the day.

Tomorrow they are going home,
So Lucy will not moan,
She will not be able to complain,
Because she will have the house to herself again.

Mark Liversidge (12)
Burscough Priory High School

THE DREAMCATCHER

The dreamcatcher hangs from my ceiling,
In the day it does nothing at all,
But in the night when nightmares attack,
The web acts like a wall.
The nightmares are tangled in the web,
And cannot escape,
But the good dreams slip down the feathers,
And into my mind they flow.
They seep through and through,
Until the morning appears with its golden hue.

Hazel Critchley (12)
Burscough Priory High School

TIGER

I'm camping in the jungle
Trying to sleep at night
There's lots of strange animals
Trying to give me a fright
What I see is different
Everything's strange and new
The sounds are unfamiliar
Unlike the things I knew

Then I hear it
Boy, do I hear it
Roaring in the night
I see it slinking through the grass
All camouflaged with stripes
It's ever so big
It's ever so fierce
Just look at those teeth and claws
Now it's chasing an antelope
It's pounced - and caught

Now it's heading for its den
I see the baby cubs
Like playful, friendly pussy cats
Not big and bad like their mum

I'm camping in the jungle
Fast asleep at night
The tigers are all happy now
They won't give me a fright.

Julia Marsh (12)
Burscough Priory High School

FOOTBALL MAD

Ryan Giggs has superb pace,
He will take on defenders in a race,
Scores a goal or two,
And will probably surprise you too.

Nicky Butt is hard,
He is nothing like lard,
Against teams he is mean,
He plays along with Roy Keane.

Roy Keane is a demon,
He plays like a mean 'un,
He scores a few good goals,
His best mate is Andy Cole.

Ryan Giggs has superb pace,
Nicky Butt is ace.
Roy Keane is their mate,
And they are United's all time greats.

Dean Blackwell (12)
Burscough Priory High School

MY BROTHER

My brother is the devil,
He acts like a clown.
He's as small as a mouse,
As loud as the traffic in town.

He's as messy as myself
And he eats like a pig.
He's as funny as a monkey
And he always likes to dig.

He's as rough as a lion,
He has play fights with my dad.
He's the nicest little brother
That I'll ever have!

Rebecca Jennings (12)
Burscough Priory High School

WHAT IS WEATHER?

What is weather?
Weather is rain
Weather is snow
Weather is wind
See everybody go.

Weather is grey
Weather is bright
Weather is day
Weather is night
Oh what a sight.

Weather is loud
Weather is quiet
Weather is thunder
Weather is lightning
It's all very frightening.

One minute bang
One minute flash
One minute cold
One minute wet
One minute golden
One minute grey
But whatever the weather, today is today.

Faye Norris (13)
Burscough Priory High School

CHRISTMAS

An excited child awakes
Early as the dawn breaks.

She looks outside and sees the snow
Runs downstairs past the mistletoe.

Decorations are hanging all around
The house is quiet, not a sound.

She sees the presents under the tree
And wonders are they all for me?

The tree was as tall as a tower
And the star on top sparkled with power.

So this is special in all children's lives far and near
I wish you a Merry Christmas and a Happy New Year!

Nicola Smith (12)
Burscough Priory High School

SKIING

First you pick up your skis.
They are waxed as smooth as silk.
The edges are as sharp as razors.
Then you catch a lift up the mountain.
It suspends like a spider on its web.
It's very quiet, all you can hear is the gentle breeze.
The snow below sparkles like 1000 jewels.
You finally reach the top which slopes steeply away.
You push off with your poles and whiz down like a rocket.
You weave to slow down but even then you're like a Ferrari
                              without brakes.
You finally reach the bottom and say 'Phew!'

Thomas Holmes (12)
Burscough Priory High School

THE HAUNTED HOUSE

I stepped into the haunted house
I was as quiet as a mouse
Creeping about!
A man came to show us our room
It was as dark as midnight on a winter's day
As small as an ant
I sat there.
I was lonely and cold
Shivering with fear.

Shadows were around me, coming near
Creaks in the floorboards
That only I could hear
Fear
Fear
Is near.

Jenny Worthington (12)
Burscough Priory High School

A STORM

A storm is as loud as a jumbo jet.
If your window's open, you might get wet.
Splishing and splashing on your window ledge,
Trickling down to the roof off your shed.
In the morning when it's wet and damp,
I wish I was in a
Holiday camp!

Lynsey Wells (12)
Burscough Priory High School

THE FORGOTTEN LAND

In the dark reaches of space,
Lies a land forgotten,
A land with a once beautiful face,
By God begotten.

The aliens there meant to destroy,
Left the planet in such a state,
Acted as if it were a toy,
Such a terrible debate.

The land was destroyed or ruined,
It's beautiful wonderful masses.
All the waste could have been binned,
But now the atmosphere contains deadly gases.

Even the places they hardly went,
Underwater, out of sight,
Soon became twisted and bent,
For no reason, not even spite.

Their evil machines,
Ploughed up the land,
Planting 'Modified' dreams,
But was luckily banned.

Soon the planet became so bad,
Horrible, twisted and bent,
That the aliens went mad
And took up their bags and went.

They left a once beautiful land,
Entrusted to them by God,
To be loved, worked and manned,
But they couldn't give a todd.

The race has gone, forgotten,
Probably ruining another place,
Leaving that now ugly planet,
Which once housed the human race.

Robert Berry (12)
Burscough Priory High School

PREDATOR

Predator he lurks in the undergrowth
Predator he sits and waits patient and calm
Predator he moves silently not a break of a twig nor a rustle of a bush
Predator as quiet as a mouse tiptoeing forward
Predator his glinting, glittering teeth come nearer and nearer
Predator I feel him come
Predator I see his gruesome, glaring eyes
Predator I start to panic, I start to run
Predator but I know there's no escape
From next door's dog predator
I am near the exit
I reach the gate
But I am too late
I felt the weight from his pounce
I try to struggle but I fall
And a fate worse than death
The dog's tongue comes out
And I am drowned in slobber!

Christopher Ernest (12)
Burscough Priory High School

SCHOOL IS OUT

School is out, teacher shouts
Children are running
Happily humming,
One child runs to the toilets to hide
One teacher sits in the staffroom and sighs
Listing the day's events in her mind.

Isabel Smith had drunk sky blue paint
She then went dizzy and felt rather faint.

Oscar had tied together Pete's and John's laces
Up they both stood and fell flat on their faces.
Tired and weary home they go,
The thought of tomorrow makes them feel low.

Kathryn McNeil (12)
Burscough Priory High School

BONFIRE NIGHT

B right flames shining
O n your way to the bonfire
N ice bright colours
F iring into the sky
I n trails on their way up and up
R iveting conversations and
E xcitement all around

N earer to the end of the night
I nside the car going home, looking out the window
G lowing red ashes on the floor
H eading home, you are sad
T hough you'll have to wait until next year.

Liam Canavan (12)
Burscough Priory High School

FROST...

It sparkles in the glowing moonlight
Crystals glitter and shimmer against the black background
Lying smoothly on the worn out leaves
Forming diamond trees and crystal leaves.

Footprints that were made that night
Silently shimmer and sparkle and glitter
Nightly creatures come out to see
Why the sparkly water won't move.

The fresh sun comes up
Warming everything
The crisp cool crystals slowly fade away
And drip and splash
Until the next time
Then leaves turn to diamonds.

Ann Dutton (13)
Burscough Priory High School

BONFIRE POEM

B ombs and gunpowder
O ff goes the rockets flying in the sky
N ight is as black as black can be
F ireworks are dangerous
I   diots are having tea
R ockets are nicely coloured
E ating toffee apples, yum yum.

Kate Mortimer (12)
Burscough Priory High School

MY DREAM CAR

My dream car is the world's shiniest silver
With gigantic, comfortable yellow leather seats
I would drive it up to 200mph
And would attract all of the women.

My dream car has glimmering spoke alloys
With a body kit 3 inches from the ground
With a big, chunky leather steering wheel
And spectacularly cool air conditioning.

My dream car has two twin exhausts
And a breathtaking 24 valve engine
And electric windows and sunroof
And talking navigation control.

My dream car also has cruise control
And it has anti-lock breaking system
Also televisions in the back on the head rests
And colourful zeon lights.

Matthew Bullock (13)
Burscough Priory High School

VEGETARIAN VAMPIRE

In 1960, a long time ago,
Lived a vampire, though not many know.
Now when I say vampire you'd usually think blood,
But unbelievably this vampire was good!

He lived in a castle that was made of stone,
But one day he got fed up of being alone.
He moved to a park to live in a tepee
And yes it's true, the vampire is a hippy!

He sings by a camp fire, he's into peace and love
And at the back of his tent he keeps a pet dove.
He never eats meat, a true vegetarian,
Instead of a bloodsucker, he's now a librarian!

Patrick Farrell (13)
Burscough Priory High School

SCHOOL TIME'S OVER

S chool's over
C rushes in the corridor
H ome here I come
O h where's my mum?
O h where's my dad?
L eft at nasty school

T ime is up
I' m walking home
M e on my own
E vening makes me
S cared but

O h here comes my mum
V ery worried
E very space looked at
R eally late.

Paul Acker (12)
Burscough Priory High School

33

ELEPHANTS

Elephants are seen in different ways:
Fat and ugly, dark as eclipse days.
But *not* me, I think they are great,
Intelligent and gentle, despite their weight.

They are as wrinkly as an unironed shirt,
To keep themselves from sunburn,
They cover themselves with dirt.
They raise their trunks in triumph and glory
And their flapping ears, now that's another story.

The baby elephants are so small and sweet,
Spending their days scampering round their mother's feet
With their short, stumpy legs, ears and tails
And loving their baths, whilst spraying in pails.

The unreal ones are said to be
Unlucky, unless facing the door
Although I can't believe they're unlucky -
I do it, just to make sure.

Jessica Newton (12)
Burscough Priory High School

MY DOG

I have a little dog which is fat,
She loves to chase, she loves to chase cats.
There are lots of dogs on our estate
Who can't wait to go for a walk,
But they can't tell their owners because they can't talk.

My dog is so fat, she's just had her dinner,
There is no point in a diet, she never gets any thinner.
She has lots of toys that make a lot of noise.
When it's time for bed she feels quite sleepy
And that's my dog Cindy!

William Dudley (12)
Burscough Priory High School

HALLOWE'EN NIGHT

H allowe'en night is fun
A ce if I say so myself
L ooking at people with masks on
L ighting pumpkins too
O ff goes witches, ghouls and ghosts
W e don't know which scares us the most
E ating toffee apples, knocking at a door
E veryone is dressing up and having fun
N ight is getting darker, frosty and cold

N aughty gremlins pinching our cheeks
I t's nice to go home warm as toast
T his is the part that we love the most
G remlins are sleeping and quiet as mice
H appy to huddle together
T rick or treating is finished for now
      B ut there's always next year look out for a *wow!*

Verity Richardson (12)
Burscough Priory High School

CHRISTMAS JOY

C andlelight shimmering on Christmas Eve
H olly-decked mantelpiece gleaming with baubles
R oast turkey cooking in the oven, ready for dinner
I mpatient children, restless with waiting for Santa
S leep at last as they snuggle down deep under quilts
T he trees glisten gracefully like stars in a velvet sky
M orning arrives at last
A nd excited voices shatter the silence
S anta has been and brightly coloured parcels lie underneath the tree

J enna lifts up the packages to see the labels
O pening parcels marked with her name
Y ells of excitement ripple through the air and

I nto the chaos of the swirling sea of torn paper
S parkling lights twinkle like diamonds

H igh on top of the decorated
E vergreen, encircled by golden beads like
R ivers of fast, flowing water
E verywhere happiness reigns.

Jenna Birch (12)
Burscough Priory High School

SPACESHIP OF S ALAVISTIE

Spaceship shooting through the air.
Hyper-drive going;
Lasers a-blare!

Spaceship speeding through space.
Fuels flowing;
Pilot flies with grace!

Baddies exploding, glittering sparks.
Fuselage blown;
He's won the war!

We've won the war!

Scott Mooney (12)
Burscough Priory High School#

WHAT LUCK WITH GOLDFISH!

There was once a goldfish named Kelly,
Who lived in a bowl on the telly,
She should have been fed,
But now she is dead,
And floats on the top all smelly!

There was a goldfish swimming round his bowl,
He wasn't young but he wasn't old,
He wasn't fat but he wasn't thin,
He wasn't fed,
Now he's in the bin!

The bowl was cracked and the water was green,
He was the ugliest goldfish you had ever seen,
He only had one eye and his fins had fallen off,
His scales were tarnished and he had a smoker's cough,
He was only five and would have made it to six,
If it wasn't for a cat named Felix!

Vikki Graves (13)
Burscough Priory High School

THE CHIPPY

The chippy is a wonderful place
Where they serve chips
With cod, haddock and plaice.

But out of them
Chips are best
Cos in fat they are dressed!

Homefries, crinkle cut, microchips too
All make wonderful
Yummy, yummy food

The chippy in Croston
Is by far the best
Cos it is

So much better than the rest!

Peter Short (12)
Burscough Priory High School

THE VAMPIRE

Vampires strike at night
Only when it's dark
They are as quick as lightning
They don't show themselves much.

They have teeth like sharp nibs
They screech like bats and my dad
They creep through the rooms of the silent house.

The flickering flames of the flinching fire in the deadly
lounge where the dog lies awake waiting for the
vampire to strike.

Lyndsey Brown (12)
Burscough Priory High School

SNOW

It snowed all day,
It snowed all night,
So we decided to build a snowman
And have a snowball fight.

We put on our hats,
We put on our gloves,
We put on our coats
And our earmuffs.

As we went through the door,
What a lovely sight,
The snow all fluffy,
All crisp and white.

We went outside,
To have fun with the snow,
It was so beautiful,
With its lovely white glow.

In no time at all,
The snowman was complete,
With a carrot for his nose
And twigs for his feet.

We were out too long
And our noses went red,
So we went inside
And straight into bed.

Anthony Upton (13)
Burscough Priory High School

ARMAGEDDON

Look there, as the first one pushes its putrid head through the dry, dying soil of this barren wasteland.

See its worm-eaten flesh and maimed face, the hell-spawn, angel of darkness.

Look now, its minions come to follow it, each one more twisted and ugly than the last.

The Legions of Darkness have risen! Nothing is safe should it dare to cross their path.

As the hordes of evil march forward, the souls of the damned rise up around them.

See how their wraith-like bodies form a cocoon of white around the creatures, glinting under the light of the moon.

Watch as the Army of Death moves onwards, surely now the end is nigh!

But what is this? The demons grind to a halt, the fire of wrath burning brightly in their eyes.

Look over there! A beam of light descends from the shining disc of the moon, penetrating the enveloping darkness.

The creatures are enraged by this, their screams enough to freeze a man's blood.

But watch! On the other side of the beam, row upon row of shining golden angels descend swiftly to the ground.

They are followed by the souls of those who were good and just in life, their bodies glowing with a strong inner flame.

As the last pair of wings ends its fluttering, the ray of light is sucked upwards, receding into the blackened sky.

Simultaneously, both armies charge, the pounding footsteps echoing for miles around.

The forces of good and evil clash in bitter combat; but as the first sword connects with shield, with an ear-splitting scream, the armies vanish.

Now there is nothing, except for the silent fall of rain, tumbling towards the Earth.

Soon, the great seas of the world will arise once again, covering the wastes with water.
Life will have another chance to grow and thrive, before Armageddon, the Day of Judgement, comes again.

Simon Dowrick (12)
Burscough Priory High School

GOLDFISH

My goldfish smiles happily
I smile back
As I watch them they swim and play
In and out of the plants
Chasing and then just stop float
They eat when they want
Sleep when they feel like it
They speed around the tank
It's an easy life being a goldfish
If I was a goldfish
I would like an owner like me
I'd speed around all day
And play all night
But what if I got a bad owner
A nasty owner
With a small tank
So I'll think I'll stay me
And watch my goldfish
And I'll stay smiling
And my fish will stay smiling at me.

James R C Bezant (12)
Burscough Priory High School

MY ROOM

'Your room is an utter tip,
It's causing me to lose my grip,'
My mother wails and tears her hair,
She sits down, leaps up, 'There's a brush on the chair!

It rivals oblivion,' she cries at me,
As she trips over the litter. I just can't see
Where the problem lies: I like it like this,
It's got atmosphere - it is utter bliss.

'There's the cap! I've asked you day after day -
I've told you - reminded you to put it away.
But still it lies there in the middle of the mat,
Just tell me dear - can you explain that?

There's so much junk on your settee,
I can't remember if it's blue or it's green,
There's no room for me to sit
And underneath there's a rotting games kit.'

But the cap belongs there it seems to me,
The kit's only been there two weeks I think reasonably,
It's convenient to have all my books on the floor.
To me it shouldn't be less but more!

It's creative, it's cosy, it's original,
I don't mind small spaces, all in all.
So what if I can't find the covers for my CDs?
Those bumps in the songs are interesting to me.

Mum points at the tissues that litter the floor,
She hurts her foot on the way to the door,
There's a pile of old washing mouldering there,
She shakes her head as she heads for the stair.

And me - I am left to contemplate,
The beauty of chaos in its natural state.

Susie Perkins (13)
Burscough Priory High School

ANIMALS

There are all sorts of animals, big and small,
There are bats, rats, horses and cats.
Cats love to jump around chasing a ball,
While rabbits really aren't bothered at all.

Humans are a type of animal as well,
Mice are small and insects are too,
But humans are small,
Just like me and you.

Birds are quite small,
They fly around all day without a care at all.
If I were a worm,
I would slither around,
But be careful to keep my head underground.

It must be fun to be an animal,
Whether it's a bird, reptile or a mammal.
So now you know just what to do,
Now don't be a fool,
Go and adopt a stray animal too.

Joanne Truesdell (13)
Burscough Priory High School

DUSK TO DAWN

Softly on the evening hour,
As the sun closes its eyes,
Little twinkling stars come out,
The silent moon lights up the skies.

Mother comes to say goodnight,
Now rest your sleepy head,
Children walk slowly up the stairs
And go quietly to bed.

Foxes dart across the lawn,
Like robbers on the run,
Birds sit sleepily in their nests,
Waiting for the sun.

As the sun begins to rise,
The birds come out to play,
Mother comes to say wake up,
It's the start of a brand new day.

Charlotte Taylor (12)
Burscough Priory High School

FRIENDSHIP

Making friends is a very good thing,
It goes through life with you.
It is the best thing in the world that you could ever do.
To have a friend that you could trust, help and comfort you
Would really make that special friend come very true to you.

Michael Shaw (12)
Burscough Priory High School

GOODBYE

The day has come,
We're being sent away like parcels from the Post Office.
Leaving Mummy and Daddy
Alone, alone!

On the train,
We wave, our tears falling like rain on the window
A long journey awaits us,
Goodbye, goodbye!

At last we've arrived,
Our new home? So unfamiliar and quiet.
Lots of strange people,
Hello, hello!

Standing around,
People staring like frightened kittens new to the world.
Someone pick me,
Please, please!

All around me strange surroundings,
Different people, a sea of faces.
I feel lost and alone,
Help, help!

Soon settling in,
But I'm still homesick, missing my mum.
I want to go home,
Quickly, quickly!

When will this war ever end?
It's gone on for too long!

Caroline Thomas (12)
Burscough Priory High School

THE STORM

The sky is cold, dark and grey,
Waiting for what's coming its way.

Tiny droplets begin to fall,
Making wet patches on the wall.

The wind gets stronger as it begins to whirl,
Blowing the trees and making them swirl.

The lightning gets sharp, harsh and bright,
Cracking open the dark sky of night.

The rain pours, the thunder crashes,
The wind blows, the lightning flashes.

Then suddenly the wind stops,
No more rainy drops.

Slowly now, the storm's undone,
The clouds open and out comes the sun.

Lisa Ashcroft (12)
Burscough Priory High School

FOOTBALL

I really, really like football,
I don't really know why,
I just think it's cool,
Just kicking the ball really hard
Straight in the back of the net.

I really, really like football,
I don't really know why,
Just sliding across the slippery pitch
And tackling other players.

I really, really like football,
I don't really know why,
Just scoring that all important goal for my team,
Just makes me feel cool in my own special way.

David Whittingham (12)
Burscough Priory High School

THE JUNGLE

Jungle, jungle everywhere,
Every step, another scare.
Trees and plants and scary things,
Birds that fly with coloured wings.

Trees so tall, the top unseen,
Places I have never been,
Monkeys, spiders, ants and flies,
It's hard to see the sunlit skies.

Monkeys watching, eating bananas,
Swinging playing on lianas,
Eyes so bright and really clear,
Not daring to come near.

Where to go, what to see,
It's all so very new to me.
Sounds so far, sounds so near,
How I wish my mum was here!

Annaly Fetherstone (12)
Burscough Priory High School

TIGER

I stare at him
He stares at me
He looks so relaxed and calm
But I am not, I quiver
And down my spine runs a shiver
His well-groomed fur brushes through the hot air
His black stripes as black as night
Like sharp blades a 'wonderful sight'
His orange fur as bright as the sun
Lights up the night for everyone
He hunts at day, hunts at night
Catches a glimpses of a hungry sight
His green eyes, his soft paws
People poach and break the laws
The tiger seems to give a sigh
As his marble green eyes stare at mine
I stare at him
He stares at me
He looks so relaxed and calm.

Kate Morgan (13)
Burscough Priory High School

THE BACKSTREET BOYS

Backstreet Boys are the best
Backstreet Boys beat the rest
I listen to their songs all the time
To them my bedroom is a shrine

The Backstreet Boys they are the ones
My favourite are the blonds
Nick and Brian strut their stuff
Not like Adam Rickett, he's a duff

Backstreet Boys sweep the charts
Leaving girls with broken hearts
Their British tour won't be beat
I've already booked my front row seat.

Keeley Sumner (12)
Burscough Priory High School

CHRISTMAS DAY

I love Christmas Day
it's special in every way
it makes me sing
and laugh and pray.

I love Christmas
Especially on the day
Presents and sweets
Every day, in every way.

I like tinsel on the tree
It makes me see
Baubles on the tree
Glowing lights you can see.

Green is the colour
Of the Christmas tree
It smells nice
Just like me.

Vikki Prior (12)
Burscough Priory High School

FOOTBALL

Football is my favourite sport,
I watch it all the time,
With players like Owen, Ronaldo, Juninho too,
The game is exciting each and every time.
Goalkeepers save the shots,
Defenders tackle, head the ball, they even sometimes score,
Midfielders pass, score and tackle,
Strikers score most of the goals.
My favourite team is Liverpool,
They score goals with players like Owen, Fowler and Camara.
Skill all the time.
Michael Owen's my favourite player,
He hits the ball like a rocket,
And it flies into the top of the net.
Football is the best sport in the world.

Andrew Aindow (12)
Burscough Priory High School

MY GOLDFISH

Goldfish, goldfish, they like to swim,
Around the bowl and right up to the brim.

They never get dizzy,
At least I don't think,
But if you don't clean them regularly,
The water can stink.

They calm us and soothe as they swim by
And make us sad when eventually they die.

Corinne Riley (12)
Burscough Priory High School

THE SUN

I once saw the sun
Peeking through the clouds,
But that is all I saw of it
'Cause soon after it went down.
I've heard that it is yellow,
I've heard that it is bright,
I've heard that it travels to Australia
During the night.

If only I could see it
For just one measly day,
I would run around with my friends
And very gladly play.

And at the end of the day
When the sun goes down,
I would have a smile on my face,
Not just a frown!

Lisa Jenkins (13)
Burscough Priory High School

SNOW

Snow is very pure and white,
If falls from the sky like snowflakes,
Children make snowmen or have snowball fights,
But when the snow melts they go home
And sit by the fire to warm their cold hands.

Graeme Ditchfield (12)
Burscough Priory High School

'R' PLAYGROUND

Children running
Children jumping
Children fighting
Children yelling

People munching
People shouting
People playing
People brawling

Teachers talking
Teachers walking
Teachers standing
Teachers lurking

That's how 'R' playground is.

Simon Barker (12)
Burscough Priory High School

HALLOWE'EN

Hallowe'en is a scream
With lots of ghosts and ghouls,
They run around the neighbourhood
And in all the schools.
They run up to your doorstep
And bang onto your door,
They shout to you *'Trick or treat'*
But of course they don't want meat,
All they want is something sweet
Just for them to eat.

So you'd better watch out,
You'd better not cry,
You'd better not pout,
I'm tellin' you why,
Ghosts and ghouls are comin' to town!

Hannah Yates (12)
Burscough Priory High School

MY IDYLLIC PLACE

My idyllic place is peaceful and calm
Where I can spend tranquil days wrapped in its charm
There would be a light summer breeze, and tall leafy trees
Which act as my own personal fan

I would bask in the sun and swim in a pool
And if I wish I would act the fool
Like a jester at court I'd have fun of all sorts

I would roll about in the freshly cut grass
I would be wild and free, like a bumblebee
And when the day ends and night-time falls
I'd be surrounded by four strong walls

Sat at home in front of the fire
Needing to rest, as I begin to tire
Like a bird in a nest, safe and warm
My idyllic place is my own little nest
Because home is the place that I like best.

Laura Disley (12)
Burscough Priory High School

COLOURS

Red is the colour of love,
Yellow is the colour of the sun,
White is the colour of a dove,
Orange is the colour of fun.

Blue is for Everton,
Blue is the sea,
Blue is for the sky
And blueberry pie.

Black is the colour of night,
Green is the colour of the grass,
Yellow is the colour of light,
Gold is the colour of brass.

Colours are great,
In the way they relate.

James Lowe (12)
Burscough Priory High School

WINTER

In the winter the wind blows,
Blows the autumn away,
The floor is painted white with snow,
Children run out and slip about and shout,
As the war begins,
Snowballs flying, children crying as they get one straight in their face.

Stuart Taylor (12)
Burscough Priory High School

LITTER

Litter, litter on the ground
Litter, litter on a football ground
Litter, litter not in the bin
Litter, litter in the street
Litter, litter round my feet
Litter, litter wherever I go
Don't bother dropping it, take it home
Litter is crushed cans
Litter is shredding packets
Litter is everywhere
Litter is everywhere.

Tom Taylor (13)
Burscough Priory High School

THE SCHOOL BUS

Every day at twenty past eight,
I run for the bus - I'm always late,
Rain comes through the roof,
The door won't shut,
When I stand up,
I have cramp in my foot,
I really don't have a clue,
Why I like the bus,
But I really do!

Victoria Blackwood (13)
Burscough Priory High School

MY COUSIN JEFFREY

My cousin Jeffrey is a naughty little thing.
He's vicious and mean, as wild as the wind.

He hits the cat and makes it spit and it goes as far as
a javelin stick.

He hits and smacks and runs away
After an hour he's ready to play.

He can be as good as Little Bo Peep, but that's mostly
when he's asleep.

I love my cousin, yes I do, but if you meet him you'll
know this poem's true!

Laura Natalie Wilkinson (12)
Burscough Priory High School

MY HAT

Here's my hat,
It holds my head,
The thoughts I've had
And the things I've read.

It keeps out the wind,
It keeps out the rain,
It hugs my hair
And warms my brain.

There's me below it,
The sky above it.
It's my lid
And I love it.

Nicola Hughes (12)
Burscough Priory High School

MY LAND

My land's a place of sea and sand
with its very own forest too.
I spend my days having a laze,
me and my best friend Pooh.
We roll and play all through the day,
until it's time to go.
Then we creep into our nest to sleep and rest
until another day of fun and play comes our way.
When it does we hum and buzz a merry tune of glee.
We hop and skip through the stream
pretending that we're king and queen.
Oh what fun we have playing the fool
in a place where laughter rules.

Elizabeth Levy (12)
Burscough Priory High School

CLOUDS!

Up in the sky all fluffy and white
A cluster of clouds is a beautiful sight
Playing in the wind, all having such fun
All keeping away from the big yellow sun
Whilst playing their games the wind they should fear
Cos with every breath the sun draws near
To the sun they are blown faster and faster
Oh no, it's too late to avoid this disaster
Sports day is ruined this year yet again
Everybody inside cos here comes the rain.

Nicola Downey (12)
Burscough Priory High School

MY POEM ABOUT A PLANT

In the garden by the shed
There lived a funny fellow
His face was green
His arms were red
His eyes were slightly yellow.

The rhubarb man we called him
Though he never talks to us
He can't because he's just a plant
And plants don't make a fuss.

Danika Kelly (12)
Burscough Priory High School

THE TIGER

The tiger slowly prowled through the jungle
looking for his next unsuspecting victim.
Then from a nearby tree, soft crackles
of leaves came when a monkey left
its tree to feed.
The tiger slowly closed in on the monkey.
Then pounced enclosing the monkey in
a cage of razor-sharp claws.

Natasha Vorley (12)
Burscough Priory High School

MY OLD DOG

My old dog likes sleeping
Now he is grey and old.
Although when you wake him he still likes to play.
He plays with a dog twice as big in weight and size.
Plus he still.likes to chase his ball.
When will he stop I hear my mum sigh.

Peter Swanton (12)
Burscough Priory High School

MY COMPUTER

My computer makes noises that
amaze me like a whirlpool of
enjoyment. It helps me in things
I do and things I write. I play on
my computer like I am trapped
inside.

Liam Hilton (12)
Burscough Priory High School

I SAW . . .

I saw animals run free among humans,
I saw birds, bees and monkeys among trees,
I saw animals but now stupid helping models,
I saw dolphins play with a ray,
I saw bears but not as rugs,
I saw lions, tigers and panthers and now I see
Cat robots playing with mechanical birds, it's not the same,
I saw Boeing 757 instead of flying saucers,
I saw everything but now, nothing.

James Slater (11)
Cardinal Allen High School

FUTURE VOICES

Looking back 1000 years

At famous people, famous faces
Some were kings, some were stars,
They've changed our lives in many ways
They've brought happiness, joy, sadness and grief.

Looking back at war and peace

Battles, fights, crusades and gore
Wicked men who want more power
Who want more land, who want more money
Misguided men who thought they were doing good,
were actually doing bad.

Looking forward to . . .

Will there be world peace or nuclear war?
Will crime rates rise? Will we live in a place with
violence and vandalism?
Will industry be as back-breaking as it is now?
Will we sit around pressing buttons
or will we be lugging boulders around in a quarry?

Looking forward to . . .

Will we be able to catch a bus to Pluto or other distant stars?
Will robots do everything in the house?
Will robots work for us?
Will science expand? Will we have the
technology to end world hunger?

Finally, we all hope for the best.

We ask God to look over us in the next 1000 years
We celebrate with big parties on New Year's Eve.
It's the end of the old . . . but the start of the new!

2000 years since the
Birth of Christ

Christopher Halsall (11)
Cardinal Allen High School

ALIEN VOICES

From Mars we come, to Earth we go,
To bring Earthlings their most feared foe,
The king of fire and hatred, sits at his throne,
Roaring for his next meal, the human bone,
The landing was bumpy, which is not a good sign,
He only becomes grumpy and roars,
'The Earthlings are mine.'
Stampeding through town and street,
Tearing houses apart,
Approaching children with a treat,
A bullet through the heart.
Two days of hell leaves Earth a ruin, families yell,
'What on earth are you doing?'
The war eventually reaches the end,
The world's destruction at the hands of men!

Michael Butterworth (15)
Cardinal Allen High School

THE MYSTERY VOICE

One night I was dreaming,
And then I heard a voice,
It said to me 'What is life like now?'
It took me a minute to think who was
Actually talking to me,
Then I said very sadly,
'This world is bad, everything is dying off
And all the animals are nearly extinct.'
I thought a minute to think what to say next,
Then I said to the voice,
'What will life be like in the future?'
But the voice didn't answer, it just sighed.
So I thought it would be bad like destruction
Or the end of the world or a power failure.

No one will ever know!

Dean Gardner (11)
Cardinal Allen High School

CHILDREN OF THE FUTURE

This is the future this is now,
you want to know how?
Well lots of generations have gone
and now there's only one.
The children, the fashion, the hip and hop
we can never stop we *are* the future.

This is the future, this is now,
you want to know how?
no more adults, teachers or fuss
no more rushing to catch the bus
no more detentions or being late for tea
it's fast food for me.

This is the future, this is now,
you want to know how?
The parents have gone
we *are* the one.
The fun has just begun
with the shining of the sun.

Laura Wilson (12)
Cardinal Allen High School

LOST VOICES

There once was a man,
Who spoke of the future,
He was an inspiration,
For the world to follow.

He talked in parks and squares,
About colour and creed,
And equal rights for all,
He campaigned for shared buses,
Parks and schools.

Whites revered him throughout the world,
But blacks saw him as a modern prophet,
As more and more whites disliked him,
He was shot, deep to the neck.

This was a voice of the future,
This was the voice of a man called King,
This was the voice of Martin Luther King,
This was the voice of a prophet,
This was a future voice lost forever.

John Helm (16)
Cardinal Allen High School

ABORTION

No one can hear me
out of sight, out of mind.
Do the right thing
and choose to be kind.
I can't stop you,
and there aren't any laws,
It's your body,
but I am yours.
I'm only small
but I've got feelings too,
Don't do this Mummy,
I love you.
I can't help it
if you don't feel the same way.
All I can do
is hope you'll let me stay.

Charlotte Murray (15)
Cardinal Allen High School

SCHOOL IN THE FUTURE

What will school be like in the future?
Will we go to outer space
Or surf the Milky Way?
Maybe we will go under the sea
And play underwater hockey?
What will school be like in the future?

What will school be like in the future?
Will we go to France
And learn the belly dance?
Or will we go to Mexico
And ride a buffalo?
What will school be like in the future?

What will school be like in the future?
Will our books have chocolate sheets to eat
Instead of paper sheets?
Or will we have to eat gruel
Instead of food that's cool?
What will school be like in the future?

Jennie Maria Bywater (11)
Cardinal Allen High School

LITTLE SHAUN

We searched all day,
We searched all night,
We searched until the morning light.
When all at once, I saw a sheep,
As little Shaun stood at my feet.

He was so tiny,
He was so cute,
He had the smallest little hooves.

With his bony
Charcoal feet,
His coat was like a shiny
White sheet.

With bright blue eyes,
which shone and shone,
It made me think
'Where do you belong?'

In a field,
Or on a plate
You will never know
What will be your fate.

Caroline Cardew (15)
Cardinal Allen High School

A WALK IN THE PARK

Do you remember when flowers filled the valley?
Yellow, red and pink. Now there's hardly any.
Walking in the park, everyone did.
Nobody's here, just one little kid.
No park to play in,
No trees to climb up.
The only thing left is a path to walk your dog on.
No picnic benches,
No indoor seats.
Trees are going down.
Kids can't climb.
I'll tell you who did this crime
We did this crime,
No one's here now, not one.
I don't know where all the people have gone.
Do you remember when people were here
All happy and jolly?
If we all work together,
We might get back
Our flowers and children
But only if we *all work together.*

Caroline Baron (12)
Cardinal Allen High School

LIFE

Life is a long, winding struggle,
times are happy and sad,
People laugh, people cry when closeness
is lost and found.

Losing people close to you, may seem
like the end of the world,
But a new life is waiting for them
above space, in a heavenly place.

New life is born and found, and a
feeling of happiness is thrown around.
It brings people closer together,
and a special bond is found to last
forever and ever.

Life is what you make it, whether it's
good or bad,
So make the most of it whilst you can
Don't waste time, just enjoy.

Gillian Blundell (15)
Cardinal Allen High School

CHANGES

The words cry out to you
yet you fail to hear.
You are lost within your hatred
and there is nothing I can do.
It is always the same
you're too stubborn
you will never change.
This time it's different
everything has changed
I give up
I'm tired of trying
and for the first time in your life
you can be the loser
for we can never turn back time.

Samantha Harvey (15)
Cardinal Allen High School

SAVE THE SEA!

The sea, sea, sea,
Is it coming? Is it going?
Only time will tell.

Are the dolphins going
The jumping, gleeful dolphins?
Save the dolphins.

Are the whales going
The tail-flapping whales?
Save the whales.

Are the fishes going
The pretty coloured fishes?
Save the fish.

Is the coral going
The pretty, living coral?
Save the coral.

Are the seas going
The very different seas?
Save the sea!

Kimberley Wright (11)
Cardinal Allen High School

WHAT OH WHAT WILL TURN OUT SOON?

Dogs, we will sleep anywhere,
Any table, any chair.
Us dogs, we don't care,
We will sleep anywhere.

What oh what will turn out soon?
The clock strikes 12 will we be doomed?
Millennium comes, what will change?
What oh what will turn out soon?

I love my food so I'll admit
Will the food change?
Could we be eating smelly turnips?
I love my food so I'll admit!

What oh what will turn out soon?
The clock strikes 12, will we be doomed?
Millennium comes, what will change?
What oh what will turn out soon?

Will we have to go to school
To learn how to write?
Do maths and English?
Will we have to go to school?

What oh what will turn out soon?
The clock strikes 12, will we be doomed?
Millennium comes, what will change?
What oh what will turn out soon?

Natalie Buschini (11)
Cardinal Allen High School

THE FUTURE

What is the future
about to bring?
Will it be all bad
or not just boring?

Have we discovered
all there is to know
about our world?
So do we now know?

Will day turn to night
and leave us in the dark
So we won't be able
to leave our mark?

So if this happens
to each and everyone
I will be very sorry
for I'll never be a mum.

So it's time to go
and leave the past
forget our life
and breathe our last.

Laura Chadwick (11)
Cardinal Allen High School

I HAVE A DREAM

I have a dream,
A dream I have
That the whole wide world will be happy, not sad.
That everyone should at least have food,
Even if you live in the Third World.

Nobody should be unkind and selfish,
But everybody should have food in their dish,
Even if you are rich and wealthy
You should take pity on the poor and unhealthy.
If you are black or white, green or blue
You should have a dream and it will come true.

Michelle Armstrong (13)
Cardinal Allen High School

LOOKING BACK!

Son: Dad, Dad, what was it like?
        What was it like?
        Was it rough, tough, quiet or nice?
        Was it loud, smoky, full of dust?

Dad: It was all of that, sometimes just at once.
        The cities were big, bigger than anywhere.
        The countryside was lovely, it was
        The smell, look, lovely it was.

Son: Where did you live Dad, where did you live?
        Did you live in the big city?
        Did you live in the countryside?
        Where did you live Dad?
        Where did you live?

Dad: I lived in a little village of Hambleton
        In the countryside, lovely that was.
        It was me and my brothers, my
        Mum was single, we were happy.
        I meet friends I still know today
        And as they say that was the good
        Old days Son, that's what it was
        Like Son, lovely it was.

Richard Turek (11)
Cardinal Allen High School

IN THE FUTURE

In the future
There are no wars
Everybody cares
Sun shines every day
Bright and orange
There's never a cold day.

In the future
No one gets upset at school
Because they're in the park
Or at the pool.

In the future
The grass is green
But purple too
The flowers are pink
But sometimes bright blue.

So now I leave the future
And head back home
As I leave the year 3000's
Own Millennium Dome.

Natalie Gornall (11)
Cardinal Allen High School

How I Saved My Own Life

Not very long ago - four years at the most.
I met a girl about my age - she said she was a ghost!
She said she was from the future: the year 2003,
And she said that in the future she knew me!
She told me when I was a teenager - 15 to be precise,
Then she gave me a lecture about what a mess I'd made of life.
She told me her name was something like Laura Cullen,
And that if I didn't listen up I'd end up in a coffin!
I shivered but pleaded 'Tell me more!'
She bit her nail and said 'Are you sure?
In the summer - just a normal day
You were invited to this party.
Your mate said 'Try this! It's cool, really!'
She said its name was Ecstasy.
You took it, then you took some more,
And pretty soon you were at death's door.
You couldn't stop - you never even tried
And then, at last, one day you died . . .'

When I was 15 these words my friend declared.
I said 'No,' she said 'You're scared!'
I said 'Maybe, but I'm alive,
If you take this then you're going to die!'
But the girl from the future - who was she?
Well Laura Cullen . . .
. . . Wait a minute
. . . That's me!

Laura Cullen (11)
Cardinal Allen High School

DAD

I'm running round my garden
at the age of five,
Suddenly I fall, great pain,
My mother comforts me,
No father.

I'm scared at night, so dark,
Strange shadows, I cry,
My mother comforts me,
No father.

First day at school, unfamiliar
faces, mums kissing and crying,
Fathers, proud and telling,
my mum stands alone,
No father.

But now I'm grown, I'm expected
to understand, my three brothers
are my only male role models,
but still I don't understand
Why?
No father.

I wonder where he is and why
he's not with me! Has he got a
whole new family while I'm left
with
No father?

I've never said 'I love you Dad.
Goodnight Dad. Why Dad?'
But I still can't tell my mum I'm sad, I have
No father.

Sarah Sumner (16)
Cardinal Allen High School

RESURRECTION UNFAILING

Life by day, death by night,
Annihilation and destruction as inner demons strike,
Our future's cold, the future's near,
Wholesome souls bow down in fear,
Tectonic plates rumble - Third World villages crumble,
Presidents, prime ministers and monarchy humble,
Where's our Saviour as clocks strike Armageddon,
A shivering discovery our hell, where's heaven?
Hell-fire and brimstone, devastation follows,
Hopes, prayers and prospects, weary and hollow.
Commandments broken, crime spreads like a cancer,
Why not change our ways? That's the answer.

Crisis, continents on the verge of being lost,
Cataclysm, premonitions, personal holocaust,
World wars no comparison, mental attributes down a level,
Prejudice, persecution the work of the devil.
No rainforest, vegetation, all wildlife fades.
Lucifer's evil warriors on mindless crusades,
Why have we done this? Population meets zero,
Parasites and hooligans crucify our heroes,
Diablos' bloodlust, nuclear weapons wind up,
Why not stop this? Make your mind up.

Silence is broken, cathedral bells sound,
Violence unopened, finally faith is found,
Harmony, tranquillity as peace fills the land,
God the Holy Spirit lays on His holy hand.
Cities restored, vitality not rotten,
Havoc, mayhem, terror, in a blink, all forgotten.
Sincerity clouds the Earth as human will is risen,
No formalities, Hades, we've made our decision.

Liam Kilgallon (15)
Cardinal Allen High School

THE TINY VOICE

As I sit here every evening,
When dusk is beginning to fall,
I sit here in my chair alone,
And think to myself as I stare at the wall.

But tonight as I sit here,
When dusk is beginning to fall,
I heard a tiny voice,
It was coming from the wall.

The voice was very tiny,
And so very sad,
And as I listened whilst deep in thought,
The things the voice said made me grow mad.

The voice was talking about its life,
And how things used to be,
And how people don't care anymore,
As they destroy our world and pollute the sea.

Everyone's so busy,
There's people all rushing by,
No one has time to stop or think,
Or to even say 'Hi.'

There are lots of posh people
Walking everywhere
Flashing their money around
They don't care.

But one day everyone will wake up
And then they will soon see
That they are destroying our world
And that they should have listened to me.

Natina Cookson (11)
Cardinal Allen High School

WHY IS IT ALWAYS ME?

Whether it's the leaking drink on the first day of school,
or an embarrassing incident as a child in a pool.
Why is it always me?

Whether it's being locked out of your computer, forgetting
an embarrassing code,
or tripping up in the middle of a very busy road.
Why is it always me?

Whether it's on holiday, being part of the 'crew'
or the gift from a dog on the bottom of your shoe.
Why is it always me?

Whether it's the fall on the unsuspecting man on the bus,
or the year learning of your high school crush.
Why is it always me?

Whether it's the unearthing of being scared of the dark,
or falling off the swings at the most popular park.
Why is it always me?

Whether it's your shopping bag crashing noisily to the floor,
or your favourite new coat getting caught in the door.
Why is it always me?

This question on my mind I cannot explain,
but however embarrassing, my whole existence seems
I just think of two things;

The first is that once a man told me,
'If people are laughing at you then
at least you are saving someone else being laughed at.'

This gives me a sense of satisfaction,
and I know that my life sure isn't boring,
for me and everybody else!

Michelle Fulton (15)
Cardinal Allen High School

What Was It Like 50 Years Ago?

What was it like 50 years ago?
These cottages used to be a big school,
Full of children and teachers too,
A big wooden gate surrounded the school,
Like a prison for kids it was.

What was it like 50 years ago?
Blackpool Tower never used to look like this,
Smaller than this a lot.
Just normal metal, not painted Climpo.
Full of playgrounds and cafes it was.

What was it like 50 years ago?
This school used to be a big hospital
Full of nurses and injured people too,
A big car park surrounded the hospital,
For people to visit their injured ones.

What was it like 50 years ago?
the moon station did not exist 50 years ago,
People could not live on the moon,
But now we can.

What was it like 50 years ago?
Cancer, meningitis, there was no cure for it,
Now hardly any illnesses exist.

Jade Wood (11)
Cardinal Allen High School

CHILDHOOD DAYS

Childhood days have up and gone,
But weary days still carry on,
Of traffic noise and smoky places
And no warmth in the bleak buildings' faces . . .

But back then, it was not the same.
Good days out often came,
Like following the crumbling hilly paths
And filling the air with shrieks and laughs . . .

Maybe swimming in the cool, trickling stream,
(Which obviously was *very* clean).
Or running uphill making echoes, loud,
Going so high that our heads touched the clouds . . .

Making dens was great fun,
And playing hide and seek in the sun,
After the holidays, go back to school,
Trying to obey the rules . . .

Childhood days have up and gone,
But weary days still carry on,
Of dangerous alleyways and delinquents' screams,
And my childhood ambitions are just shattered dreams.

Madeline Reed (11)
Cardinal Allen High School

WAR, WAR, WAR

War, war, war
it no longer exists
the world's no longer being torn apart
by war, war, war.

War, war, war
we're glad we got rid of it,
people do not get killed
because we got rid of war, war, war.

War, war, war
we are now at peace
weapons have now vanished
no longer at war, war, war.

War, war, war
no more fights to speak of
no more evacuations
because we got rid of war, war, war.

War, war, war
no more killing
no more bombing
no more war, war, war.

War, war, war
we're glad it's all over
we're glad there isn't any fighting
aren't you too?

Michael Wright (11)
Cardinal Allen High School

NEED

The need is great.
The greater the need, the harder the day.
The harder the day, the tougher life becomes.

Try a replacement . . .
. . . It would never work, it's not the same.
Find a new way . . .
. . . Too dangerous to change.
Find one willing, find a good one.

Feed your need.
Drug for buzz, buzz for drug.
Ask . . . No!
Become starved, pride and dignity is kept.
Feed the need.

The need can't be fed.
The need *is* . . . 'I want.'
I want, can't have, I want is denied.

The simplicity of a taste,
The complicatedness of me.
The need is great.

Caroline Reid (16)
Fleetwood High School

DANCE

The party was alive
Dancing and prancing
Swinging and spinning
Bobbing and frolicking
Hopping and gambolling
Playing and jigging
All night long
Screaming and shouting
Laughing and crying
Puffing and huffing
All night long
Glaring and swearing
Messing and fighting
Blazing and flashing
Sparkling and glistening
Glowing and shining
Gleaming and beaming
All night long.

Leah Rendall (14)
Glenburn High School

DREAMS!

Dreams are very special things,
That float above my head.
They come to me at night,
When I'm asleep in bed.

Bad dreams are called nightmares,
They make me feel hot.
Good dreams are everywhere,
They make me smile a lot.

But when morning comes,
I lie awake in bed.
Thinking of all the dreams,
That float above my head.

Claire Dreha (13)
Glenburn High School

PLAYGROUND

In our playground there are people who:
    shout, scream and call,
    articulate, chat and communicate.

In our playground we see people:
    bolting, running, darting, dashing and
    speeding across the playground.

In our playground we:
    walk, go across our playground.

In our playground we see:
    pushing, shoving and driving.

In our playground there is:
    fighting, bullying and arguments too.

In our playground we:
    bounce, jump and hop.

In our playground we see people:
    eating, chewing and having a good time.

Anita Clegg & Anita Buckley (12)
Glenburn High School

CONCERTS

Loud, ear-splitting,
deafening, piercing
to the ears.

Roaring, screaming,
yelling, shouting
from one's mouth.

Pushing, shoving,
driving, bashing
into each other.

Gossiping, chit-chatting,
small talk, news mongering
to one another.

The concert is finally over,
people are saying how -
excellent, fantastic, first-class, first-rate
and great it was.

Samantha Williamson (12)
Glenburn High School

ICE-CREAM

I like ice-cream a whole lot,
It tastes good when days are hot.
On a cone or in a dish,
This would be my only wish.

I don't like vanilla, it's too plain,
My love for mint brings me pain.
Choco, malty and saucy mango,
Randy raspberry makes me tango.

Tutti-frutti tastes so good,
Rum and raisin's in my blood.
A heaven's dream is toffee ripple,
One little lick makes my legs cripple.

Put them all together, my body'll give way,
I could eat ice-cream every day.
My fetish for ice-cream is so strong,
Stick with ice-cream and you won't go wrong.

Natasha Crangle (13)
Glenburn High School

IN THE PARTY

In the party there is dancing
with hopping and twirling
and swinging and swirling
and bouncing and leaping
and jumping, no sleeping
with spinning and springing
and prancing and singing
And that's what a party's about.

With screaming and coiling
and shouting and calling
whirling and swaying
hopping and playing
with music and jigging
vaulting and ringing
And that's what the party's about.

Quickly gets faster with
swanking and rocking and bolting
and cavorting and ducking and diving and
That's what the party's about.

Krista Morgan & Tanya Curran (14)
Glenburn High School

WINTER

Red noses,
Cold bones,
Shivers and shakes.

Dark nights,
Closed curtains,
Wind blowing outside.

Roaring fires,
Steamy teas,
All warm inside.

Ice on the windows,
Slippery paths,
Ponds and puddles,
Like sheets of glass.

Scarves and mittens,
Duffels and hats,
Keep the icy winds away,
And the snow and rain,
From ruining the day.

Dark mornings,
Snuggle deeper into bed,
Pull up the covers,
I'd rather stay here instead.

For someone has been busy,
All through the night,
Jack Frost is his name,
And he's made the world white.

Laura Elms (13)
Glenburn High School

THE WORLD IS FOOTY MAD . . .

Adams
Beckham
Cole
Dixon
Edmundo
Fowler
Grimandi
Hyppia
Izzet
James
Klinkladze
Leonardo
McManaman
Ngotty
Owen
Petit
Quinn
Ronaldo
Shearer
Thompson
Unsworth
Vieri
Westerveld
Xavier
Yorke
Zidane.

Mark Newby (13)
Glenburn High School

LIVERPOOL FC

Liverpool are a very good football team,
They have won many honours before
Roy Evans took over.
Now we have Gerard Houllier,
Who is a very good manager.
We have a great striking force,
Robbie Fowler, Michael Owen and
Titi Camara, they are all good players.
Our midfield is good but need to pass,
Their defence are OK but need stamina.
Our goalkeeper Sander Westervald,
Is brilliant but needs to calm down.
This is Liverpool Football Club,
A very good football team.

Stephen Bristow (13)
Glenburn High School

THE GOBBLER!

He's big and tall,
He'll scare you all,
He'll gobble you up,
And drink your blood from a cup!

Five eyes and five feet,
Walking down your street,
He wants you to play,
But don't go out today!

So here's a word of warning,
To all people out there,
Beware,
Of the gobbler!

Stephanie Dreha (13)
Glenburn High School

REVENGE

Before they go into battle
The colonel shouts 'Remember why you're fighting! Good luck.'
He turns his horse and rides to safety
Halfway
And the men who led
Are dead on the floor.
The ground
Thumps
With the cannons,
Soldiers cry for help,
So much bloodshed.
The enemy!
They start running.
They meet
Swords crashing, clanging, crying,
The thump of the cannon, lightning and thunder.
An explosion!
The ground they stand on is gone.
One soldier gets up,
His brother is dead
And five enemies are coming.
Vengeance!
He draws his sword and runs at the enemy
While screaming his rage.
He runs, turns, twists, rolls.
Only one enemy is still breathing, crying in pain.
He looks at his sword,
The weapon that killed four men.
He looks at the still breathing enemy.
Four men is not enough.

Philip Finegan (14)
Glenburn High School

THE MERSEYSIDE DERBY

At the derby,
A capacity crowd,
Big fat men,
Shouting loud.

On the pitch,
The tackles were hard,
At half-time,
Came 2 red cards.

The second half began,
The whistle loud and clear,
Owen nearly scored,
Very, very near.

Jeffers was fouled,
He positioned the ball,
Then curled it,
Round the Liverpool wall.

The game ended,
And the Everton fans cheered,
Then went to the pub,
For a load of beers.

Ian Smith (12)
Glenburn High School

PARTY

The party is jumping
Dancing, prancing
Hopping, skipping
Swirling, swaying
Swinging, spinning
Bobbing and rocking

Fighting and swearing
Bouncing and shouting
Laughing and talking
Noisy and
          lonely.

Toni Bell (14)
Glenburn High School

SCHOOL

Why do we have to go to school?
Whoever thought of it was mean.
But I can bet you any money in the world
That he was over 18!

Maths, science, English and French,
They're all rubbish to me.
The only lesson that's slightly good
Is the best lesson, PE.

Now, uniform is another story,
I mean, is it meant to make us look smart?
It always gets wrecked anyway
In boring lessons like art!

When I ask people what's their best part of school,
It will always be the same as mine,
Actually it's not even a surprise,
It has to be *hometime!*

Colin Malone (13)
Glenburn High School

FAIR

Fair, fair, fair
What do I think about the fair?
I think joy
I think fun
I think fast
I think pop
I think slop
I think banging with clanging
I think screaming and wheeling
I think lasting and passing
I think yelling and bellowing
I think long
I think song
I think riot
I think quiet.

Hollie Gelhardt (12)
Glenburn High School

SCHOOL

The bell rang.
9.
It's school time.
Pupils rushing, pushing,
squashing, squeezing,
running, dashing, charging.
Lesson time.
Chairs clattering, banging,
crashing, champing,
bumping, stamping,
rumbling, bashing, blasting.

Michelle Wearing (14)
Glenburn High School

HORROR

Horror is gruesome,
Horror is great,
Horror makes my eyes gleam,
It doesn't make me shake.

Horror is the night-time,
It's the creaking of the floor,
The things under your bed,
The shaking of the back door.

Zombies, killers, ghosts and knives,
Chopped off arms and cut out eyes.

Blood and guts must drive you nuts,
But there's nothing better than a dark scary wood,
With lots of blood, it makes me feel good.

Kimberly Rowlands (13)
Glenburn High School

OUR PLAYGROUND

Swearing, glaring,
Tearing, baring,
Clapping, tapping, slapping, napping,
Stamping, tamping, chanting, panting.

The playground roars!

Beaming, screaming, leaning, teaming,
Screeching, preaching, reaching, teaching,
Chatting, patting,
Laughing, snapping.

This is our playground.

Helen Dumkow (12)
Glenburn High School

ONE SPOOKY NIGHT

One spooky night
Tonight, tonight.

The spooky spiders bit
Spooks and ghouls come out to fight on Hallowe'en night
Tonight, tonight.

The pumpkin glows with all its might
To give the children a great big fright
Tonight, tonight.

All the children have a good night
Tonight, tonight.

They all went to bed for a good night's sleep.

Ian Rendall (11)
Glenburn High School

MY TEACHER IS A MECHANICAL MACHINE

Red, flickering eyes,
He knows when you're telling lies,
Clattering and rattling,
Ear-splitting and deafening,
Yelling and bellowing,
Calling and roaring,
Thinks he's first-class,
First-rate and great,
He's not artistic or
Brilliantly gifted,
Thinks he's main,
But he's just insane.

Victoria Miller (12)
Glenburn High School

WITCH'S SPELL

Lait fo a yeknom
Rae fo a gip
Eson fo a god
Dum fo a gip.

Riah fo a namuh
Tops fo a eson
Pird fo a pat
Hsalps fo a esoh.

Foow fo a gorf
Walc fo a raeb
Seye fo a twen
Spil fo a gorf.

Siht is a lleps taht is lla
Sdrawkcab.

Natalie Duggan (12)
Glenburn High School

THE FIGHT

Bashing and biffing
and bopping and hitting
and clouting and boxing
and plugging and slamming
the fight keeps going.
And slogging and smashing
and striking and walloping
and jabbing and knocking
and thumping and tugging
all night long.

Shaun Neve (13)
Glenburn High School

MUM

To my dearest loving mum
Thank you for all the things you've done
All the things you do for me
Now I realise, now I see
Through all the rough and all the good
I know the things I do, I should.

Don't you worry because I'm here
There's no need to shed a tear
I'll try not to let you down
I'll even try and hide that frown
For things I do may be wrong
You're always cheerful, full of song
You're my mum so tender and dear
I'll love you forever, I'll make that clear.

I know that there's only me and you
I love the things that we both do
I'll be there forever more
Because you're my mum I do adore
Now this poem is finally done
It's from the heart, I love you Mum.

Helen Pulford (13)
Glenburn High School

GHOSTS

Ghosts can go bump in the night,
Ghosts can sometimes give you a fright!
Ghosts can also give you a scare,
It can sometimes lift up your hair.

Monsters are big and hairy,
Also they are very scary!
They are sometimes ugly and green,
Monsters can also make you scream.

Adam Waite (12)
Glenburn High School

THE WAVES

The waves
are crashing, bashing,
swinging, swaying,
rippling, rushing,
drifting, smashing,
racing, roaring,
calming and calming
until they reach
the shore.

Anthony Hoy (12)
Glenburn High School

THE WAVES OF THE SEA

The waves of the sea are
drifting, sifting,
dipping, diving,
clashing, dashing, slashing,
mashing, crashing, bashing,
ripping, rushing, roaring, racing.

Stephen Borrows (12)
Glenburn High School

A Very Rich Pocket!

In a rich person's pocket what did I see
A lot of expensive things just waiting for me.

A gold Rolex watch which still told the time
A very big bubblegum flavoured with lime.

All his credit cards were with his money
And a white handkerchief which said 'I love you honey'.

Then I noticed an old wooden pipe
Next to a couple of plane tickets
Which I was ready to swipe.

Jenny Hays & Gemma Harrison (12)
Glenburn High School

The Trolley Trip

The trolley's wheels clatter, stutter, bang and clatter
The children bellow, roar, call and cry
The parents foot it, advance and hoof it,
The kids are shrieking, screaming, screeching and squealing,
The staff are stacking, clamping, rocking and massing,
The children are scrapping, barking, grazing and scuffing,
The parents are talking, chatting, cracking and conversing,
The kids are playing, sporting, frisking and competing,
The staff are selling, wheeling, dealing and trading.

Nikki Shaw (12)
Glenburn High School

COMMON ROOM

Shouting
screaming
dancing
jumping
crawling
brawling
dawdling

bored
scored
floored
screaming
crying
calling
yelling

Dinner time
gossiping
saying
fighting
striking
biting

whistling
hooting
clapping
banging
scrapping
dripping
dropping

on the common room floor.

Vincent Bennett (12)
Glenburn High School

PEOPLE ARE . . .

People are tall
People are small

People have long hair
People have short hair

People are black
People are white

People are nice
People are nasty

People are polite
People are rude

People are different
Which one are you?

Samantha Baxter (12)
Glenburn High School

SPACE

The moon is round
The sky is black
The stars are twinkly
I'm sure about that.
The sun is bright
And Mars is red
There's life on Earth
But is space dead?

Amy Hedges (12)
Glenburn High School

MY BROTHER

My brother Kevin is not quite eleven
In and out he plays
On long, hot summer days
On his great big bike
Oh what a little tyke.

Teatime comes around
Kevin can't be found
In he comes flash and bold
Mummy says
'Your tea's gone cold!
Up the stairs
Straight to bed
Before I make
Your bum turn red!'

Rebecca Harrison (11)
Glenburn High School

THE FOOTBALL MATCH

Kicking, diving, running, dashing, jogging, marking,
Working, moving, diving, booting, steaming, fouling,
Unjusting, marking, yelling, shouting, calling, pointing,
Dealing, communicating, screeching, clapping,
Sliding, winning, on the football pitch.

Kev Dean (12)
Glenburn High School

GHOST

There once was a ghost named Paul
Who went to a fancy dress ball
To shock all the guests
He went quite undressed
But the rest couldn't see him at all.

Lisa Stacey (12)
Glenburn High School

SOUNDS OF A RABBIT

My rabbit Thumper he thumps and bumps
the clattering of the hutch
the rustling of the hay
the crunching of a carrot
on a cold winter's day.

Sarah Nixon (11)
Glenburn High School

POEM OF SAM KELLY

Slippery Sam slithered on the slippery floor.
She tried to get up but she slipped some more.

Try as she might she put up a good fight,
But she slipped, slithered, slipped some more.

Samantha Kelly (11)
Glenburn High School

THE TRAIN

The man was waiting hours on end
Until the train came round the bend.
He jumped out and onto the train
He banged his side and squealed in pain.

Hiding in the luggage bay
Until the guard walks past he'll stay.
When the guard walked past he ran
Straight into the ticket man.

'Come on, please pay me this time
And if you don't you'll pay a fine.'
'But please, I can't pay you at all.'
'So then I'll have to make a call.'

I looked straight out, the cops were near
I stepped right out and shook with fear.
Off I went in the cop car
To the station which seemed so far.

It was dark and gruesome in this cell
It was like something out of hell.
It was so scary all night long
I shouldn't have done it, it's so wrong.

I'm very stupid I stepped out of line
And now I'll have to post my fine.
I'll get home, buy a stamp and lick it
Next time I'd better buy a ticket.

Daniel Anderton (11)
Morecambe High School

MILLENNIUM FEARS

Outside the joyful buildings,
A storm was drawing near,
I could hear the bangs of thunder,
As my heart stopped dead with fear.

The great huge storm cloud in the sky,
Spelling death upon us all,
A huge black panther ready to pounce,
A blanket ready to fall.

Inside, a different story,
Happiness everywhere,
But the anticipation and excitement,
Was far too much to bear.

Ten seconds to twelve,
The countdown begins,
The countdown to the end,
The end of a year, the end of a life,
And maybe the end of a world.

Outside again there's thunder,
On every number down from ten.
And rain pelts down in buckets,
With hail now and then.

Five seconds to twelve,
The countdown continues,
The countdown to the end,
The end of a year, the end of a life,
And maybe the end of the world.

'*Happy New Year!*' the people cry,
The blanket splits, moon and stars shine through,
A fresh new hope, fills my heart with joy.
It's not the end, but the start of millennium new.

Pamela Slack (12)
Morecambe High School

THE CURSE OF THE MILLENNIUM

The curse of the millennium,
Strikes at midnight.
And the darkness seems to stretch,
For hours on end.

As you wake and get ready for parties,
With family and friends and folk you don't know,
You must remember the curse that strikes,
Computers and TVs have no hope in sight.

And as you are partying,
You feel something's wrong.
The computer alas,
Is broken, gone wrong.

The curse you see has no mercy,
For those who did not heed the warning.
TVs fail, computers crash,
And the fire's gone out,
Leaving a heap of ash.

That is the curse of the millennium,
Take care in case another should come.
Remember the curse shows no mercy,
And all microchips are gone.

Kathryn Glover (12)
Morecambe High School

YOU AND ME

Your eyes are the blue lake in an alpine wood,
Your lips are as soft as a peach in the morning dew,
Your hair is the bark of the trees you climb,
Your arms are as strong as golden chains.

My heart is a safe, sturdy tree,
My love is a dog, true by your side,
My eyes are the green trees that surround your lake,
My hair is the roots that hold the trees.

We are an alpine wood, together,
We are trees to climb, together,
We are as true as a dog, together,
We are as strong as a chain, together.

Divided, the alpine wood is felled, apart,
Divided, the safe trees fall, apart,
Divided, the dog is dead, apart,
Divided, the golden chains snap, apart.

Claire Flower (12)
Morecambe High School

WORLD WAR 1

Wheee! Boom! Boom!
The fireworks of death explode,
In the trenches, the screams,
As the death sentences hit the mud,
Men were drowning, trying to climb out of the sludge,
Some in a violent fit, were climbing over the top.
One man lay buried in the mud.
I reached out and touched his outstretched hand,
He was as cold as ice,
As dead as a doornail.

All was calm, like still water,
All was black, night was here,
A brave soldier got to his feet,
He climbed over the top with a football under his arm,
A few followed.
The Germans joined in, and an hour of peace followed,
One of the officers found out and stopped it,
But it gave me a different view on life,
I hated the world I lived in,
And looking at the crippled deformed teenagers,
I thought many others did too.

Katy Henderson (12)
Morecambe High School

THE GHOST SHIP

The moon was a smear underneath
The shadows of cheerless clouds,
The sea was bloodshot with violence,
And the night sky seemed polished with soot.

Over the horizon I witnessed
A shimmering glowing image,
She had the figure of a ship,
Lying gracefully upon the sea.

Her sails were like a maiden's hair,
Gliding high in the night sky,
Her masts were like outstretched arms,
Her body was opaque and dull.

Suddenly a glittering light
Illuminated her path,
Then she slowly faded away,
Diving back into the raging sea.

Jessica Uphill (12)
Morecambe High School

SCOTT'S FINAL DIARY ENTRY

The night was black as coal,
and the wind blew chill like ice,
my fingers and toes were blue with cold,
I must find shelter tonight.

Snow driving as hard as diamonds,
hitting my face and eyes,
Burning skin red as crimson,
The lace-white floor and skies.

My quest for the pole is driving me on,
the will to win is great,
Pushing me further than I have ever gone
I must increase my pace.

The cold is biting like a dog,
my heart is getting weak,
I must prepare to meet my God,
and find eternal sleep.

Scott.

Kylie Chapman (12)
Morecambe High School

THE CRY ON THE MOOR

My voice echoes across the empty, barren moor,
Like a gust of wind,
Along the emerald grass it carries,
Over the treetops it soars,
It reaches the city and still doesn't stop.

My prey hide in hollows deep underground,
Thinking they're safe, safe as sound,
The sun is a burning star,
My cry reaches there too.

It is not a cry of happiness,
But one of sorrow,
I am the voice,
I am the lone wolf.

Laura Hodgson (12)
Morecambe High School

SWIMMING

My heart pounded with excitement as I stepped
onto the blocks
The starter raised the starting pistol
Take your marks!
I pulled back on the block
All was silent and still
The pistol fired
My hands released and my legs pushed
diving streamlined into the cool, inviting water
I broke the surface of the water
The race had begun
I dug into the water with my arms
My legs kicked furiously and my heart beat rapidly
I approached the wall at maximum speed and
pulled my body through the turn
This gave me the speed to burn
Hearing the muffled screams and cheers
of the spectators
I took my last breath and extended my stretch
and swam into the wall
Turning and looking to see how I had done
I won.

Laura Devey (12)
Morecambe High School

THE MILLENNIUM BUG

I am the millennium bug!
Tick-tock tick-tock!
I have come to ruin your parties!
Tick-tock tick-tock!
Only another two minutes to go!
Tick-tock tick-tock!
Time is passing extremely slow!
Tick-tock tick-tock!
Only another one minute to go!
Tick-tock tick-tock!
This is going to be a blow!
Tick-tock tick-tock!
5 . . . 4 . . . 3 . . . 2 . . . 1 . . . !
Now the time has come!
Ha! Ha! Ha! Ha!

Ben Hill (12)
Morecambe High School

GRANDAD

One hot sunny day in July
You were out doing your shopping.
God decided to take you away
And now you are free from pain.
We pray you didn't suffer Grandad
Cos you were all alone.
We never got to say goodbye
On that hot sunny day in July.

You're now in God's paradise
Looking down at us from above.
You're always in our thoughts Grandad
We think of you with much love.

So life must go on for us now
Because that's what you would have wanted.
We'll cry and smile and never forget you Grandad
Goodnight, God bless, all my love.

Amanda Howard (12)
Morecambé High School

MILLENNIUM

In the millennium will computers crash?
Will tides rise and land disappear?
Will the world end? Will quakes arrive?
Will volcanoes blow their tops?
When will we die? Will our bodies decompose?
Will we be decapitated by passing Virgin trains?
Will films come true and will we be invaded by Martians?
If life exists out there, will it be our ally or enemy?
Will people die of starvation in the Third World?
Will war break out?
Will a hero save the world from devastation?
Will we live in fridge-freezers?
Will we discover time travel and travel to Roman times?
And travel in flying cars?
Will organic food get out of hand?
And will plants have brains?
Will people be immortal?
The millennium's soon,
Let's hope the end isn't!

Peter Donald (12)
Morecambe High School

COUNTDOWN

100 days from the day I first write,
Next year will be seen in a brand new light,
Now 90 days till the bug bites,
Technology has reached a brand new height.

Only 80 days left till the end of the year,
Only 70 days left till the millennium is here,
Only 60 days left till everyone can cheer,
Only 50 days left till computers should fear.

Now 40 days left to go,
People out there had better know,
That in computers the bug might show,
With 30 days left, the lights are low.

What if the Millennium Bug is here to stay?
With 20 days left we can only pray,
Used to be 10 left, now it's only 1 day,
I know one thing the new year's coming our way.

Rebecca Owen (12)
Morecambe High School

THE COMPUTER

I am your path to all knowledge,
I have pictures galore,
I am a library alone,
My hard drive are the bookshelves,
My memory is the books,
I swallow your files and hide them safe,
In my brain I see news, I see war,
I hear gossip, I need more!

I can be naughty by shutting down while you're unaware,
I destroy your files and fail to save,
I am unstoppable,
I cannot be defeated . . . until . . . until you pull the plug.
My lights go out quicker than a fox,
My screen goes black, darker than the night,
My mind goes dead until another day,
Then I'll wait until I can lure you in!

Ben Henderson (12)
Morecambe High School

LEFT OUT

People sneer
People laugh
People hit
People walk away
What can I do?

Nothing

Nothing at all

I can do things
Not as much as other people
Just like the guy on a bonfire
People standing
Staring
Amused
Where do I belong?
Where can I go?
Where is this place?
I wish I was there!

William Gordon Mackenzie (13)
Morecambe High School

MILLENNIUM

At the end of December '99
There will be an event for once in my lifetime.
People will gather from far and near
To fill our land with thanks and cheer.
Events will be staged at venues all around,
The most famous is the Dome in Greenwich Town,
Which will open its doors to
Bring in the new,
At 12 o'clock for all to view.
Countdown starts at
Number 10,
9, 8, 7, 6, 5, 4, 3, 2, 1, like a
Spaceship taking off,
Here it is the second
Millennium.

Adam Ball (12)
Morecambe High School

THE SEA'S BATTLE

I watched as the waves rumbled ashore
Like an unstoppable army mounted on their horses
The sea spray threw knives at my face
Each one stung more than the last
All of a sudden there was an almighty blast
Screams filled the air
Wave after wave entered the battlefield
Still the coastal cliffs would not yield
Protecting the shore like a giant shield
Wave after wave gave up and turned away
To return and fight another day.

Rachael Stansfield (12)
Morecambe High School

THE WOODCUTTER'S DAUGHTER

Here I stand by day and night
Waiting for the sun's light,
Waiting for the woodcutter's daughter,
But here I am feeling the slaughter.

O' lady who owns my heart
Surely you are my missing part.
With your hair as curly as the tree branches
But here I am in one of your trances.

Oh my love have pity on me,
As I watch you in the arms of Wiliby
My heart is broken with a crash,
How could you be in the arms of that ass?

Marching, marching, marching went my heart to the foe,
As my mind shouted 'Wiliby stop, she's mine, let go.'
My mouth did not, and my feet stood still.
My eyes began to fill.

Then there was a creaking, sliding sound,
As the door moaned across the ground.
and there out stepped the woodcutter's daughter
With her hand gripped tightly over her supporter.

The gun, so cold, was an ice cube in my hand,
I closed my eyes and shot with a bang!
My heart stopped as I saw Wiliby still standing by the door,
It was the woodcutter's daughter's blood on the floor.

And here I stand by day and night,
Waiting for the sun's light,
Waiting for the woodcutter's daughter,
And so she stands my beloved haunter.

Amy Quesne (12)
Morecambe High School

WHERE AM I?

Walking through the streets,
The cars are flying high.
There's music all around me,
Where am I?

There's people in the street,
I sit down and sigh.
Can this all be true?
Where am I?

High-pitched laughter,
Tall buildings reaching to the sky.
I can see people flying,
Where am I?

The clock strikes twelve,
People shouting, 'God save her.'
Three thousand and nine,
I'm in the future!

Helen Snape (12)
Morecambe High School

IN THE FUTURE

In the future
Will we be here?
Will Earth be gone?
Will we move on?
Will we have to die?
Will we learn to fly?
Will we live on red-hot Mars?
Will we fly in little green cars?
In the future will we live amongst the stars?

Joe Moulton (12)
Morecambe High School

THE CUPBOARD'S SECRET

The cupboard stands in the room,
No one knows what's inside,
Some say it's going to open soon
But they have always lied.

One day I walked into the classroom,
The cupboard door is locked.
A noise I suddenly hear, could this be my doom?
I run to the classroom door, it is locked!

I skip, I run, I jump to the window,
It does not budge.
I feel as small as a tiptoe,
Someone must have a grudge.

I sit in the centre of the room
Crying on the inside,
My head full of doom,
Will I ever feel the warmth of the sun on my side?

The hours tick by
As I am trapped in this room,
Suddenly I hear, I hear a horrible cry
Doom! Doom! Doom!

The cupboard doors open
Like an eagle's wing.
I hear the words spoken
'Will you come in.'

Without a thought
I enter in.
I am suddenly caught
In a forever spin.

William Birnie (12)
Morecambe High School

THE FUTURE OF CARS

Cars now are dirty and smelly
As they rip up the ozone layer.
They are destroying the world as we know it.
Every day off they go, squirting out their poisonous gases.
The noises that cars make, are *brrr, vrummm, cruuum* and *thllum.*
But the future looks bright for cars, electric cars and solar-powered cars.
They are clean and green.
They make the future look bright for our world.
Our world is fading away unless we do something near this day.
But our world is fading, fading, fading.

Carl Southam (12)
Morecambe High School

FIRST DAY AT SCHOOL

At the first day of school
I wasn't very scared but I was prepared
To do all those lessons that day.
I got to the gate and I felt like running away,
First lesson was art, we had to paint.
It was a very big school and very old.
When I was running to the dinner queue
I tripped and hit my head.
The last lesson was geography, that was good with Mr Ledward,
And that was the first day at Morecambe High.

Paul Spencer (12)
Morecambe High School

WAR

Dodging the fireworks that boom above my head,
I ran back into the mud pit full of plague
that I was living in and had been living in for over a year,
It seemed like a decade.

When the war is over I will be running home
to my family, to my life.
That's if I live that long without going over the top.
My friend and I watch the sky at night,
as clear as a newly-cleaned carpet,
until the fireworks start again, then we fight.

Jessica Perry (12)
Morecambe High School

THE CRASHING SEA

The sea is a crystal
All the fish jumping and swimming,
The fish are like little germs in a body.
The sea rushes up the beach,
All the little starfish sitting on the bottom,
Crashing on the dark grey rocks,
The storms thunder and lightning,
On the poor little boat,
The boat is like a needle in a haystack.
Now the storm is at an end,
The sea goes back to its crystal.

Matthew Whitaker (12)
Morecambe High School

BULLYING

Bullying
Bullying like a hammer hitting down on you.
It never stops.
It blows down on you, and you can't get rid of it.
It never stops.
You can run but you can't hide.
It never stops.
It's a cover engulfing you and you cannot get from underneath it.
It never stops.
Strike after strike, blow after blow, it tears you apart.

It never stops!

Gary Howard (12)
Morecambe High School

THE TITANIC

On that fateful night in 1912,
When thousands of people died,
That tragedy on an unsinkable ship,
That left families and loved ones outraged.
From the dockside the Titanic looked as big as the world,
But when it got out to sea, from its decks it hurled,
Some people were rich,
Some people were poor,
But only a few were kept from death's door.
The ship hit an iceberg as white as a ghost,
The story of which we will hear of the most.

Lindsey Rodmell (13)
Morecambe High School

THE KITTEN

Bewildered at birth,
The clumsy kitten wanders round like a drunken fool.
Each tiny paw hits the ground like a feather floating, lightly
to the floor,
And its tail is a spinning pendulum out of control.
Time goes by like a drive down to the local corner shop,
And the almost tame tiger-like creature is a pie or a cake rising.
Growing.
Fascinated by bits of blue string,
Torn like hairs from our heads,
And as it scatters at every loud sound,
It is an ant fleeing from a waterlogged home.
But at last the time that every living thing goes through,
It's old and weary and all it does is sleep and eat,
Until it pops.
It doesn't feel the need to run,
And either way sometime it will come,
It feels OK but then it's gone,
Dead.
Its heart starts thumping slower and slower,
Until it eventually *stops* . . . like a broken watch.
Where time,
No longer,
Exists.

Holly Lupton (13)
Morecambe High School

WHAT DO WE KNOW?

There are deep, dark, strange and nasty
secrets in the staffroom
when the teachers escape at break
from the confines of the classroom
what's behind the staffroom door?

There are a thousand cups unfinished
all covered in green mould which looks
like mushy peas gone cold.
Coffee stains and rings remain
where they have overflowed.
Piles of files and unmarked books
and last term's lost reports look like
they've been dragged around the tennis courts,
the PE teacher's sweaty vest and
lycra cycling shorts.

There are paper planes and brown tea stains
from last night's staff meeting.
This place is a downright disgrace
not fit for even a pig to eat in!

There are deep, dark, strange and nasty secrets
in the staffroom.

Katrina Rudrum (12)
Morecambe High School

THE MANY FACES OF ME

Lazy and warm like a lion in the sun,
Chasing a cotton reel just for the fun,
I move like a shadow, silently at night,
I chase the birds and give them a fright.
Who am I?

I am a tiger, I'll pounce on my prey,
If you have any food I'll definitely stay.
A bouncing ball from ceiling to floor,
Keeping away from the dog next door.
Who am I?

Guess who I am and then you will see,
These many faces are what makes up me!

Sarah Hill (13)
Morecambe High School

THE SEA

The sea has to be one of the most powerful things on Earth,
Sometimes it's as calm as the night,
But other times, it's as rough as two men in a boxing ring,
On a sunny day the sea is like a blue rug on a washing line,
Gently and softly
Blowing like the nice, neat overlapping waves of the sea.
The sea to me has to be as beautiful as a rose,
But as clear as the clearest thing in this world,
But maybe as dark and gloomy as the night.
The sea is a royal blue shining, shimmering dress
That the Earth is very proud to wear.

Laura Ashcroft (12)
Morecambe High School

MILLENNIUM 2000

The year nineteen ninety-nine,
Next year's gonna be fine,
We're going to wine and dine,
The pleasure's going to be mine.

The Millennium Dome is gonna be seen,
When the millennium's gone away and been,
I wonder if the Millennium Bug's mean,
What will the millennium do for the Queen?

The millennium is now here,
So why not have a few beers,
I'm sure you're gonna have cheers,
Lots of people will have tears.

The millennium has gone and passed away,
It is now just like another normal day,
The millennium has gone like tides at bay,
People everywhere will have something to say.

This is going to end,
My message I will send,
The bug is round the bend,
This will now be the end.

Lyndsey Briggs (12)
Morecambe High School

FUTURE VOICES

The people were frantic running about,
The people were queuing to enter the Dome,
It was as white as a snowball, as big as the moon,
Although no one knew what was coming soon.

The people all scattered into the Dome,
I just strolled in so sad and alone,
The computers growled like a man in terrible pain,
All along it acted just like a brain.

It stored information just like a book,
You could do and play so much,
It looked like a robot so much energy used,
It could do so much it was up to you to choose.

I looked at the screen to see what to do,
I wanted to go on the Internet too,
I placed my hand on the plain, still, white mouse,
And then I suddenly saw a gigantic house.

I turned around to see everyone busy,
Some children were running making me dizzy,
I turned back to see a plain black screen,
What had gone wrong, was I in a dream?

The lights had gone off like at night I suppose,
People stood still as if they had to pose,
I shouted to people the bug has arrived,
They just ran and ran and set off to drive.

If only they knew what I really meant,
It was a waste of time and money spent,
Just for the Dome which the bug had attacked,
The Millennium Bug, The Millennium Bug.

Rachael Horn (12)
Morecambe High School

WAR

The General gives the shout,
The troops go running,
Running, running,
The troops go running
Out to their doom.

The enemy is in sight,
The soldiers start shooting,
Shooting, shooting,
The soldiers start shooting
And then sneak in.

The first line are down,
The troops sneak in and hide,
Sneak in and hide, sneak in and hide,
The soldiers sneak in and hide,
And wait for the second.

Behind enemy lines.
The second line appear from nowhere,
Nowhere, nowhere,
The second line appear from nowhere,
And spot their victims.

Gunfire breaks out,
People are screaming,
Screaming, screaming,
People are screaming
Before they fall down.

And so the screaming continues,
And won't ever stop,
Ever, ever, ever,
It won't stop ever
Until the suffering stops.

Joe Robinson (12)
Morecambe High School

THE FLOOD

We're not in the Millennium Dome,
It's sixteen times the size of our home,
Thousands of burglaries all day long
Whilst we're singing that beautiful song.

All the computers crash and blow,
All the rivers start to flow,
It turns to dust and really thick ash,
It's turning the people to moulding mash.

No one knows that the computers crash,
Even though they'll soon be ash,
It starts to rain,
And floods the drain.

Now only one quarter land,
Will England still stand?
No one has noticed the flood
Apart from the people who are blood.

The whole world is water,
Even the woman's daughter,
There's nothing here today,
Why did it end this way?

James Hurst (12)
Morecambe High School

Party Time!

It's nearly here, it's nearly here,
The millennium party,
We're all getting dressed up,
We all look like princes and princesses,
Well maybe not!
When we get there the music goes,
Boom, boom, boom.
Everybody gets up to dance,
It looks like they've got ants in their pants.
The food is on the table,
Yum it smells nice,
There's an array of colours on the table,
Everything from sausage rolls to quiche.
The clock goes tick, tock, tick.
The clock strikes twelve,
And we all sing 'Auld Lang Syne'.
The millennium's here and everyone's excited,
New things to see,
Everyone's excited, it's here.

Olivia Shorrocks (12)
Morecambe High School

The Worst Day Of The Week

Wednesday night came around too soon,
I sat in the corner of my room hiding.
I could hear the *splash, splash, splash* of water
Like a waterfall in the Amazon.
The floorboards creaked with footsteps heading
to my room,
The shadow was a haunting ghost,
There was a shout to my room, 'Bathtime!'

Gemma Boon (12)
Morecambe High School

MY CAT!

My cat is the most funniest cat
that you did ever see,
Her fur is rough, not nice and soft
like cats fur ought to be.
She costs me lots and lots to keep,
her food is very dear,
Of fish and milk and bread and that
she will not even hear.
Five pound last week,
one pound before that,
Don't you think she's the most unusual cat?
When I give her money she always says
'Thanks.'
I think I ought to tell you now,
she's just my savings bank.

Zeen Hadi (12)
Morecambe High School

THE BEACH

I go to the beach every Sunday because everyone
Goes back to school on Monday.
The sand is like blazing sun,
The sea is like a blue mirror and the sky is like a jewelled carpet,
The sun shines all day long,
We build sandcastles one by one,
We eat ice lollies, they are yummy, then we go and bury Mummy,
We jump the waves, they are so high, then we surf to the sky,
We ride the donkeys for a pound, they make an hee-haw sort of sound.

Sarah Kellett (12)
Morecambe High School

RUNAWAYS

Charney was a beautiful dog,
For she was white and fluffy.
She had two puppies
Which were named Tarney and Bobby.

They lived out on the cold streets
And though Charney tried to keep them warm,
She did nothing but fail,
All they seemed to do was squirm.

Bobby and Tarney were always playing games,
But they weren't happy out in the cold,
So they ran away
To a cottage in the fold.

The owners there took them into warmth,
The two dogs were happy there.
The owners treated them well,
They had no need for fear.

The puppies seemed to be content,
But there was something missing.
One day on the dogs walk
It became clear what they were wishing.

They saw their mum lonely and sad,
Instinctively they ran to her,
Happy and full of joy,
'Okay we'll take her in,' said the owner!

From then on, for the rest of their lives
They all stayed together,
And lived peacefully
In the small cottage forever.

Nikki Asghar (12)
Morecambe High School

IN THE RING

The sly fox and the bloodhound fight it out,
The blood drips from the cuts and wounds,
He stands up so hot and sweaty,
The sound he makes so fierce and ferocious,
No one gets in his way.

The tangy, twisty fox throws a punch,
And knocks the bloodhound down,
But the bloodhound gets up as quick as Roadrunner,
Speeding swiftly, soundly along,
No one gets in his way.

As the referee counts, 1, 2,
Suddenly the sly fox gets up like a spring that's just
been made from the factory,
Amazed the bloodhound gets a shiver down his spine,
No one gets in his way.

Like a hero the sly fox fights back,
The blood and sweat drip from his mouth,
And the wobbly tooth hanging by a root,
The bloodhound falls to the ground, the ref starts to count, 1, 2,
No one gets in his way.

Suddenly the crowd go quiet,
The number 3 came out and the sly fox wins.
As the crowd go home the bloodhound closes his eyes,
The sly fox is the number one sly animal,
No one gets in his way.

Adam Nutt (12)
Morecambe High School

ALIEN MILLENNIUM

Straight down from Venus they came,
alarming and frightening
the people
like one gigantic game of risk,
green people came out of a spaceship taxi,
then the music started,
glaring
the green people formed a dainty conga,
aliens dancing all over *our* globe,
the people begin to join in
bringing food and booze,
everyone is dancing,
everyone is singing,
everyone is happy
and peaceful,
then the green men disappeared
but no one noticed . . .
everyone is having too much fun,
everyone woke up drunk the next day
and they thought it was just
one big dream.

Vikki Sole (12)
Leyland's St Mary's RC Technology College

MARTIN

Boys, boys, boys,
Some boys are stupid,
Selfish and unkind,
Most boys that is.

One boy however
Stands out above the rest,
I usually see him out and about
Only with the best.

That's the boy that I adore,
The one that Heaven made.
He's the one that stops
My heart beginning to fade.

One day I'll get the guts
To tell him what I think,
But until that day I think I will
Leave him on the brink!

Lisa Ferris (13)
Leyland's St Mary's RC Technology College

ANOTHER WORLD

Why are half the world rich,
and the other half poor?
Why do we moan about the rain
when for some it's the difference between
life and death?
Why do we want designer clothes
when they want anything to keep warm?
Why do we drive for a mile
when they have to walk fifty?
Why do we moan about our jobs
when they depend on charity?
Why do we argue with our families
when they would give anything for someone to love?
Why do we laugh
whilst others are crying?
It's another world outside what we see,
give them a hand,
give the world a hope for the millennium.

Laura Berry (14)
Leyland's St Mary's RC Technology College

WAR AND PEACE!

Why can't the whole world be at peace?
We fight about money and rights,
Why does the world fight with each other?
Why don't we make peace?
Watching the news is so depressing,
So cancel world debt throughout the nation,
Cancel all environmental hazards,
Save money for the Third World countries,
Send food and clothes to the poorer countries,
Give to charities,
Let justice be brought to Earth.
Why watch other people suffer?
Why watch them starve and die?
Why watch their families suffer?
Why can't we see that the world is full,
Full of cruel, shallow-minded people?
Could we do something about it?
Together the world could sort out all the problems of debt,
We, together could also sort out the consequences of world debt,
Then this world would be a better place for everyone,
Everyone would be friends and we could all celebrate the new
Millennium together in peace.

Jessica Miller (13)
Leyland's St Mary's RC Technology College

MILLENNIUM

The millennium is soon to come,
And so many things have not been done.
This will happen once in our lives,
But so many things to organise.

As the day draws nearer and nearer,
To celebrate the end of the year,
We will have parties and loads of fun,
Inviting everyone to come,
12 o'clock the clock strikes midnight,
We all scream with all our might.

Charlotte Woods (13)
Leyland's St Mary's RC Technology College

THE CODE OF AN ANT!

To serve the mighty colony
And obediently do as I am asked,

To put effort in my digging
And never ever give up,

To contend against enemy troops
With anger and great confidence,

To treat each and every ant
With great individuality,

To resist any bullies and cowards
And stand up for my rights,

To practice in dodging the vicious feet
Of the inconsiderate humans,

And if all these tasks are completed
I will pass as a
fantastic ant!

Marie Harman (13)
Leyland's St Mary's RC Technology College

MY PET

I have a pet hamster,
Hovis is his name,
He is white and beige,
And looks cute in many different ways.

He is my hamster,
He lives in a cosy cage,
He hides in his house
For most of the day.

But at night
He emerges from his bed,
Stretches his little legs,
And makes his way to his water pot.

When he's wide awake
I open his lid and say 'Hi,'
Every night I place him in his ball,
And he runs like mad around the hall.

While he's out and running round,
I clean out his bed and cage,
On Saturdays I change his bedding,
So it's comfy and clean for the week ahead.

I can stroke him a lot,
But he jumps when I try to pick him up,
He only stays in my hands for a while,
I think he's scared I'll hurt him.

I love him like mad,
He's the first pet I've had,
And if he went away,
I would cry.

I'd probably get another,
But none will be like Hovis!

Gemma Kenyon (13)
Leyland's St Mary's RC Technology College

TURNING POINT

Green to gold, rusty red,
the leaves are falling on my head,
on these cold days I wish I could,
stay cosy and warm in my snug bed.

Crispy brown leaves under the trees,
jiving Jennies in the breeze.
Blackberries and elderberries hidden in the bushes,
pears fall off trees as the wind rushes.

Those long summer nights are now forgotten,
as bonfires roar, summer is turned out of the door.
Then,
When everyone else is sound asleep, the sly old fox goes,
creep, creep, creep.
Softly
stealthily at the dead of night,
the little pheasant is to have a fright.

The fox smells his prey,
and stalks to the hay,
an eerie sound pierces the sky and a
squawking bird is about to die.

Maria Jakulis (13)
Leyland's St Mary's RC Technology College

DEATH

I'm going to die,
I don't know when, where or why,
Maybe I'll be run over by a car,
Or even covered in hot, boiling tar.

I'm going to die,
Please don't cry,
Maybe I'll be executed,
Or even electrocuted.

I'm going to die
Because I'm just a normal guy,
Maybe I'll be burned in a fire,
Or even strangled by wire.

I'm going to die,
Bye-bye,
Maybe I'll be eaten by Madonna,
Whatever I'll be a gonner.

I'm going to die . . .

Philip Scarisbrick (13)
Leyland's St Mary's RC Technology College

MY LITTLE SISTER

My little sister is such a pain,
She is always looking in the mirror because she is so vain,
She gets anything she wants and it goes her way,
But she never listens to what I've got to say,
Everyone thinks she is cute but that is very wrong,
They don't know what she is like at home.

Laura Carmichael (12)
Leyland's St Mary's RC Technology College

DOGS

Dogs can be thin but some can be fat,
Some dogs raid bins and others chase the cat.
Some dogs can be clever and others may be thick,
Some dogs are healthy and some dogs might be sick.
Some dogs can be black and others might be white,
Some dogs go strolling through the dark night.

Puppies are cute, they'll do you no harm,
But if you are cruel to them they'll nip your arm.
Puppies are tiny and will play all day,
Puppies always get their own way.
The only bad thing about having a pup
Is if you don't like clearing puppy poop up.

Dogs are friendly and would be your friend,
When you need someone to talk to a dog would be there till the end.
Some people say that dogs are not nice,
If they would get one they would see they're not right.
So if you're in need of someone to play with
Go to the kennels and get a dog playmate.

Most dogs are clever and know what they want,
Sometimes when you give orders they pretend they can't.
When you're in danger they know and get help,
They would probably do this by giving great yelps.
So when you think your dog has gone deaf
It's not, it's because it can't be bothered with itself.
                    Woof,
                         Woof,
                              Woof.

Clare Howard (12)
Leyland's St Mary's RC Technology College

THE STORM

Black clouds flocked over the crowded city.
Rain started to pour down, it got heavier and heavier.
People were scattering into bus shelters to escape the pouring rain.
Rain.
Then suddenly a *bang!* A bang of thunder,
and then a streak of lightning across the sky.
Rain, rain, rain.
The boats in the harbour bobbed and swayed
with the strain of the rope.
The drains were overflowing with the pouring rain.
The river was rising swiftly.
Rain, rain, rain.
It then overflowed, a surge of water flooded the now deserted streets,
Rain,
Rain,
Rain.

David Howells (12)
Leyland's St Mary's RC Technology College

ODD

War is odd
A battle to kill others
A skirmish
The survivor wins
The winners survive
It must be wrong
Satan's job
A stamp of guns
Boom! Boom!
Hundreds in rows
All in white
Little remembrance.

Peace is odd
It's never happened
There's always violence
Death is to come
Death makes you care
It's there, not nowhere.
The Hydron's red
The sea is blue, black and green
Nothing changes
Someday maybe, someday
'March!'

Brian Sole (13)
Leyland's St Mary's RC Technology College

THE FUTURE

What future is there for the young?
So many songs to be sung.
Will our lives bring us happiness
Or will they be a terrible mess?
Many fashions there are to see,
we do not know who holds the key.
When is technology going to end?
How many e-mails will we send?
There are many hungry people about,
It makes us want to scream and shout.
The millennium is soon to come,
there are many things to be done.
What will we do when time runs out?
I'll have no worries, no troubles, no doubt.
But so far our lives are good
they are blooming like a delicate rosebud.

Claire Dewhurst (13)
Leyland's St Mary's RC Technology College

THE STARS

As I walk into the spaceship
I think about the stars
I wonder what it's like to live on
Jupiter, Saturn and Mars.

I think of the people
living on Mars
maybe next to aliens
driving in hover cars.

Then what would it be like
to travel far, far away
going on moon beaches
sitting on Mars' bay?

Big, white-headed aliens
thousands of little green men
with funny and weird names
like Zool, Zarg and Ben.

Then as I enter the spacecraft
I suddenly got scared
what if something went wrong
in space no screams are heard.

As I took off from the launch site
I felt a slight rumble
I felt like a bee
you know the ones that bumble.

As we entered space
and left Earth's atmosphere
a red light began to flash
oh God Lord, Oh dear

A fuel tank had blown, we were floating in space
and then I woke up, what a dream to face.

Peter Scott (13)
Leyland's St Mary's RC Technology College

STARING INTO SPACE

Every night I look into the sky,
All those stars so very high,
The stars further than we can see
All unaccounted for in the sea of space,
How do we know they are there?

The stars are just like pinpoints of lights
Lighting the darkness of space,
I look,
I look into space, the vastness of space,
It must be infinite for there is no limit.

Some people look to space for answers,
For calm,
But I just look to stare,
Stare through the clouds,
Through the vastness of space.

Daniel Fitzgerald (13)
Leyland's St Mary's RC Technology College

ELSA MY CAT

E   is for Elsa my lovely cat
L   is for lazy, she sleeps on the mat
S   is for soggy, when she's out in the rain
A   is for alert, for dogs are a pain.

M   is for mischievous, she is every day
Y   is for yarn with which she likes to play.

C   is for cowering when she has been bad
A   is for anger, she hates my dad!
T   is for tremble when she visits the vet.

All of these things spell 'Elsa my cat'.

Emma Johnstone (12)
Leyland's St Mary's RC Technology College

MY CRAZY POEM

In my crazy universe
There is a crazy galaxy
And in that crazy galaxy
There is a crazy world
And in that crazy world
There is a crazy country
And in that crazy country
There is a crazy house
And in that crazy house
There is a crazy bed
And in that crazy bed
There is a sleepy ted.

Loren Harrison (12)
Leyland's St Mary's RC Technology College

ANIMALS!

All animals should be treated the same
Great or small, wild or tame.
From galloping horses to friendly dogs
From chattering chimpanzees to leaping frogs.

Wild animals are the greatest of all
Especially bears that stand so tall,
Tame animals are important too
Even if they don't do what you want them to do.

The environment effects wild creatures,
So don't drop litter, listen to your teachers!

Animals die from litter being dropped
So put it in the bin after you've shopped,
If an animal is in danger, what do you do?
You call the RSPCA that's who!

Nicola O'Keeffe (13)
Leyland's St Mary's RC Technology College

HOMELESS SKY

Hi I'm sky,
My mum and dad left me,
They never said bye.
Me and my brother's lives are lame,
Although sometimes I think he's too tame.
I can't believe I live here,
In shops I can't even afford beer.
My brother has a teddy called Mandy,
However, I suggested the name Sandy.

Adam Tree (12)
Leyland's St Mary's RC Technology College

ALIEN MILLENNIUM

The party started as pops and bangs,
The music was becoming loud.
The aliens landed with clicks and clangs,
They'd wondered what they'd found.

Their dark green skin, their big blue eyes
Had frightened all the people.
All the children sobbed and cried
The rest looked through their pupils.

Then all the people heard a noise
Coming from one of the aliens.
'Sorry we frightened all the boys and girls
We're just a bunch of aliens.'

The people decided to let them join in
Seeing as how they were so swell.
They decided to dance and drink
When one of the aliens fell.

The aliens danced to the tango
Each grabbing a partner to help.
When the tango changed to the Conga
It caused the dancers to yelp.

The party finally came to an end
When one of the drunken aliens said,
'It was very nice to be your friend
But we have to go home to bed.'

Stacey Dunne (12)
Leyland's St Mary's RC Technology College

FUTURE

A bright new future we all crave
It's a new millennium
Keeping promises we have made
New thoughts and inspirations.

Celebrations will be planned
For the new millennium
Champagne will flow across the land
Goodbye to old, welcome new.

The Dome is the awesome creation
Structured for the millennium
Built from imagination
New age, wonderment and joy.

The birth of Christ we celebrate
In the new millennium
Amidst all this we can contemplate
A brand new day that's dawning.

Charlotte Watmough (13)
Leyland's St Mary's RC Technology College

THE MILLENNIUM BUZZ

The millennium is coming and what will it bring?
Fashion's not fashionable and food not rational.
Witches and warlocks, crimes and horror shocks.
Robot-driven train, acid rain.
Pencils will go, computers will know.
Computers galore, E-mail and more.
Everything will be fun, wool will no longer be spun,
All because the millennium has begun.

Catherine Neville (12)
Leyland's St Mary's RC Technology College

THE MILLENNIUM

The millennium is coming,
And wars are still going on.
People are being judged,
By the clothes they put on.
The party in the Third World,
Must come to an end.
Then we would be at peace,
And friends in the end.
People would live,
And few would die.
No frowns, no crying,
Just smiling happy faces
The millennium is here,
The wars have all stopped.

Louise Moon (12)
Leyland's St Mary's RC Technology College

MR WOOD

I have a friend called Mr Wood,
He is a ragged piece of wood.
There are rough edges here and there,
On my fingers there are splinters everywhere.
He lives in my pencil case
Along with my pens and pencils.
He is my friend Mr Wood,
What would I do without him?

Paul Boxall (12)
Leyland's St Mary's RC Technology College

HEAVENLY

As I look I see;

H er face was bronze in colour,
E very detail was beautiful and dark, dark brown,
A dventurous were her dark black eyes,
V aguely staring into deep space at times,
E ven when inside she's hurting,
N ever do her wide, bright eyes look sad,
'L ife is a gift' she whispers,
'Y ou live it, and you are never sad.'

'H eaven,' she murmured. 'Is a new home, is a new home.
E ven if you've lived your action filled life,
A nother peaceful life is waiting,
V iolent may your life be,
E very day counts in your life,
N ever will you feel violence again,
L iving in this different world,
Y our dreams are waiting for you.

H ope is up here in this world,
E ndangered you will never be,
A fter pain you relax and sleep,
V aguely dreaming about this world,
E ndless will this dream go on,
N ow I will
L et,
Y ou follow me.'

Nicola Cowley (13)
Leyland's St Mary's RC Technology College

THE MOON

Walking out into the open
looking into the sparkling sky
I see the moon shining
brightly
And I wonder - why?
The moon was conquered by man
a long time ago
But now -
what is happening to the moon
up there in space
all alone?
Does the man in the moon have
company up there?

Daniel Crook (12)
Leyland's St Mary's RC Technology College

THE RAINBOW

The sun came shining out of the sky,
And there was a strong warmth all around,
But all of a sudden the sky went brown,
As the stormy rain came tumbling down,
In buckets they came,
But all of a sudden it went amazingly tame,
Then the sun came out and a rainbow I saw
And my smile went from ear to ear.

Katie Forshaw (14)
Leyland's St Mary's RC Technology College

RUN FOR MY LIFE!

I ran through the dark,
Followed by a hunter.
I was afraid and scared to death,
I was running from an eight foot monster.

I heard the owls hooting,
Rats running through the grass.
The thing rustled through the bushes,
And sent me flying back.

It reached its broad arm towards me,
With sharp black horns on its head.
It had eight eyes on its big ugly face,
I was sure to end up dead.

Then it spoke politely,
And said its name was Bob.
He gave me a firm handshake,
And sat me down on a log.

He grabbed me by the shoulder
And beat me to a pulp.
He put me in his shiny mouth,
And swallowed me in a gulp.

I floated off to Heaven,
They told me I was dead.
But they wouldn't let me in,
So I went to hell instead.

Gary Beardsworth (13)
Leyland's St Mary's RC Technology College

MILLENNIUM

I wonder what the millennium will be like?
Futuristic cars and futuristic motorbikes.
I wonder if they will find a new planet
That has green and yellow aliens on it?
I wonder if the world will end on New Year's Eve?
Then all the aliens will rule the world
When all the people will leave.
I wonder if the aliens will let you do as you like?
Eat junk food galore with all your wildest dreams and more.
I wonder if the aliens won't let you go to school?
Then all the little children will be complete and utter fools!

Luke French (12)
Leyland's St Mary's RC Technology College

MILLENNIUM PARTY

P   artying into the year 2000.
A   ll night long you
R   ave and dance,
T   ill the sun comes up.
Y   elling, 'Happy New Year.'
I   nviting everyone to come.
N   early there, counting down.
G   igantic roar at midnight.

Rebecca Duxbury (12)
Leyland's St Mary's RC Technology College

HEROES OF THE DAY

On a Sunday slowly we walk, thinking about the game ahead.
In we go to the smelly changing rooms, smelling of last week's socks
and mud with the slight smell of sweaty boots.
Already the opposition are there and I notice the enormous centre
forward towering two feet above the rest.
I see players as big as wardrobes.
We get changed quickly and noisily.
The captain comes and psyches us up, singing and shouting
'Come on lads.'
We walk out feeling strong
ready to win a game of football.
The captains go up
'Heads' ours shouts.
He wins
we kick off and battle . . .
. . . and battle
Goal!
The end of the game draws near
'Peep!'
We've won.
We walk back to the changing rooms
and sing in the showers
for hours . . .
. . . and hours.

Simon S Taylor (12)
Leyland's St Mary's RC Technology College

SPACE IN THE MILLENNIUM

Far, far Pluto we travelled and found a creature
This creature we saw
we named Pluto
That's space in the millennium.

Neptune and Uranus, both very funny places
How did they get their names? Because it certainly suits them
Their blue and yellow fairy dust rising above the surface of the planet
when our big moon boots sink into the surface
That's space in the millennium.

Jupiter and Saturn, we travelled there too
We found another creature with furry fur and gigantic feet
That's space in the millennium.

We sent another probe to Mars and when it came back
It brought some funny goo
This funny goo we placed in a container
But started to change shape
That's space in the millennium

Mercury and Venus, we still haven't seen
I wonder
I wonder
The things we could find there . . .

Chris Woodward (12)
Leyland's St Mary's RC Technology College

MILLENNIUM

What is the millennium?
What does this mean?
Is this to celebrate the
birth of Jesus?
Or is this just a chance
to celebrate?

It is a time for celebration parties
champagne and fun.
It's only if you get really old
that you'll see another one.

When January 1st appears
will it all be the same?
Will electricity go out
and computers shut down?
Will planes go plunging
to the ground
and will people be the same?

Anything could happen
the world could blow up.
The world could change
dramatically.
What do you think?

This is a big turning point
in our lives
to some of us it's a big
occasion,
to others it's just another day
and they're not bothered when it comes.

If you think about the millennium
it is really concealed and cryptic
sometimes we don't understand
How
   It
     All
       Began . . .

Patrick Marsden (13)
Leyland's St Mary's RC Technology College

ENGLAND 2006

Come and see England in 2006.
In Wembley Stadium taking free kicks.
You will see Cole, Owen and Beckham too
And Alan Shearer scoring a few.

Watch David Seaman jump left and right
And see the England manager jump up with fright
The referee will do a trick and then the players will give him stick
You hope the opposite team will go offside
And see the England manager crack his sides.

The half-time whistle goes and you are so depressed
Because now the England squad is not at its best
Beckham is tired and Owen's not as fast
And the way the games going the crowd's not going to last.

The second half starts and you want England to win
However, you know there is a chance your hopes will go straight
in the bin
Beckham and Owen come out and they are better than ever
You just hope the final score will be as hot as the weather.

Owen starts running down the middle, Beckham says 'Pass' and
starts to dribble.
He's nearly there just a few more paces
Let's hope he can score and put the other team in their places.

He's scored, we've done it at last, we've won
The champions again, we've done it, we've done it!
It has been so long but it has been worth the wait
Now we are all going down to the pub to celebrate.

Rachael Bradshaw (13)
Leyland's St Mary's RC Technology College

THE BIG MATCH

I went to one football match,
Supporting PNE,
I saw the Tangerines score a goal,
And that's what really bugged me.

The goal went bang,
And in the net,
The scorer ran off,
The defenders were in a sweat.

The manager thought they were a disgrace,
At half-time he moaned at such a pace,
The players said 'It ain't our fault,
Our defence were as tight as a bolt.'

As they ran out for the second half,
A stupid supporter streaked with a scarf,
The police got him off,
The game carried on,
Blackpool scored 4 goals,
But the ref didn't count one.

All of a sudden we were on the attack,
Cartwright got the ball,
He buried it in the sack.

We went wild,
So did Moyes,
Everyone was pleased with the boys.

After the game, we weren't happy,
We know who to blame,
Keeper Tepi.

Christopher Cowburn (14)
Leyland's St Mary's RC Technology College

I HAVE

I have a big family

2 sisters
4 brothers
5 aunties
3 uncles and
2 sets of grandparents to be exact

I have lots of pets
1 dog
1 cat
1 rabbit
3 fish and
3 sea monkeys to be exact

I have lots of friends
1 Gemma
1 Liz
2 Amandas
1 Holly
1 Raonaid and
1 Racheal to be exact

oh and . . .

I have lots of homework!
Science
Maths
English
French and
Spanish to be exact.

Rose McClarty (13)
Leyland St Mary's RC Technology College

WARNING FROM AN ALIEN

I was walking down the street
On Earth one sunny day,
And bumped into an alien, standing in my way.
'Ligabog' he murmured with a move of the arm.
'Hello' I answered, 'I mean no harm.'

Without warning lasers shot out from his hair,
And projected pictures into thin air.
I saw this strange community out in space,
A different type of world, an unusual race.

Flying saucers and weird hairdos
Is what I expected to see,
But there were only humans, like you and me.

But something that frightened me in this case,
There was a lot wrong in this awful place.
Litter scattered along the floor,
Piles and piles building up even more,
The sounds of broken glass like a baby's scream,
Many violent wars like an unwanted dream.
It was a terrible sight, this was no joke,
You couldn't see for all the smoke.

Why did this alien come?
To show me this state,
No time to clean up now, it's much too late.
I asked the little man what it all meant,
Why was he here? Why was he sent?

'You're the future voices,
You've the key of what to do,
Time can't change it, it's up to you!'

Joanna Cassidy (12)
St Mary's Catholic High School, Blackpool